"If you're seeking freedom in love and in life overall, *The Right Combination* is the faith-builder and guide you need. Barbie and Richard share their story of surrender and redemption with complete transparency, giving you freedom to move beyond shame or embarrassment to own your story. Grounded in God's Word and heart-stirring questions to prompt your own process, this book will empower you to seek God first, to trust him, and to stay full of hope for whatever God has for you."
Tiffany Hendra, founder of The Coaching Sanctuary™ and former lead on *The Real Housewives of Dallas*

"*The Right Combination* is written with just the right combination: permeated by Scripture, purposed through pain, and penned by trusted friends. We're so glad this resource is now available to empower those on marriage 'next' with blended homes."
Shannon and Cindy O'Dell, senior pastors of Brand New Church

"Richard and Barbie Armenta take readers on an incredible journey of love, faith, and marriage done God's way. By candidly opening up about their imperfect lives and their up-and-down relationship, the Armentas show us on a very personal level how trusting in God is the only way to succeed, not only in marriage but also in life. Whether you are single, divorced, or married, this book will inspire you to seek God's purpose for your life, your relationships, and, ultimately, your marriage!"
—Ed and Lisa Young, pastors of Fellowship Church and authors of New York Times best seller *Sexperiment*

"Richard and Barbie have an amazing story to tell on issues the church isn't talking about nearly enough. Their experience and testimony will impact a huge portion of the population today because they not only talk the talk but walk the walk."
—Brandon Hensley, president and cofounder of Team Impact

"Inspiring. Thought-provoking. Challenging. This remarkable book is a must-read for all Christian couples contemplating marriage after divorce. Barbie and Richard Armenta write with honesty about the challenges of finding love, blending their families, honoring God, and waiting for his timing. You'll laugh out loud, wipe a tear, and find answers within the pages of this book. *The Right Combination* should be in the resource library of every church and Christian counselor. Don't miss it!"

—Carol Kent, speaker and author of *A New Kind of Normal: Hope-Filled Choices When Life Turns Upside Down*

THE Right
COMBINATION

THE Right COMBINATION

FINDING LOVE AND LIFE AFTER DIVORCE

BARBIE & RICHARD ARMENTA

Kregel
Publications

To our big, beautiful, blended family.
We are so grateful for your love, support, and encouragement.
We appreciate your willingness to let our story be heard.
We love you!

CONTENTS

Acknowledgments 11

Introduction 13

Part 1: Two Lives . . . One Spark

1. Richard and Barbie Yahoo! 17
2. Where It All Began: Richard (Part 1) 25
3. Where It All Began: Barbie 38
4. Where It All Began: Richard (Part 2) 53

Part 2: The Decision Before the Decision: Comparing Notes with Barbie and Richard

5. Who Am I? 69
6. Life Renovation 81
7. You Be You and I'll Be Me 99
8. The Walls Come Down 112
9. Comfortably Uncomfortable 122

Part 3: It's All Happening

10. Worth the Wait 139
11. And Two Become One 158

ACKNOWLEDGMENTS

TO OUR AMAZING FRIEND Debra Caffey. Thank you for the countless hours of listening, editing, writing, and encouragement. We appreciate your sharing your gifts and talents to bring our story into the world. We could not have done this without you!

Special thank you to my dear friend Sue Baldwin (December 31, 1960–January 26, 2019). My life and my family's lives have been forever changed by your willingness to share Jesus. I want to always honor you by giving away what you gave to me.

INTRODUCTION

GOD IS A GOD WITH A PLAN. The Bible tells us, "He has made everything beautiful *in its time*" (Ecclesiastes 3:11, emphasis added). In today's world of instant gratification, we want what we want, and we want it all now. Faster downloads, groceries delivered in an hour, swipe-right dating—anything and everything is available at our fingertips, and we're upset when it's not. So waiting through a process, waiting for a plan to unfold—no one has time for that!

The Right Combination is our story of learning to really live and love again after divorce. It's a journey of God's grace and redemption, of how God took our choices to be obedient to his call on our lives and made something beautiful from our broken pasts. It starts with my husband Richard's decision to surrender everything to God, and it shows the power one simple choice can have to positively change the lives of others forever. It is our story of how God took Richard and me from our individual messy places and directed our steps toward one another to create something neither one of us was ever sure we could have in a relationship.

Most of my recollections come directly from the pages of my personal journals, words I thought nobody would ever read, in the hope that you will be inspired in your own journey to find the kind of love God wants for you despite your life's imperfections—not just the love of a mate but the love of God and love for yourself. I relived many of the emotions and pain of the days I wrote the entries as I searched through them for the threads that bound Richard's story and my story together into *our* story. It may not be the most vulnerable thing I've ever done, but it's up there.

I would never have been able to experience all that I have without the willingness to believe that if I want to *be* something different, I have to *do* something different. Sounds easy, right? That is, until you are challenged to actually put it in practice. Doing what it takes is hard, and it requires us to get out of our comfort zone, go against what we know, and make new choices. Sometimes those choices are uncomfortable or unpopular, and we find ourselves being the odd man out. It might feel like the biggest risk you will ever take. But take it from Richard and me: it is so worth it. True freedom comes through doing; it comes from making a new decision and taking the first step.

Each chapter tells you a bit of our story and what we went through in learning to live and date God's way. At the end of every chapter, we challenge you to begin your own process. Through these pages, we share Scripture to encourage you in God's truth: you are worthy, and it is never too late to have the abundant life God wants for you. Richard and I share lessons we learned along the way in hopes of inspiring you to know that if we can do it, you can do it too. We also pose some questions to get you thinking about who God made you to be so you can freely embrace all he has planned for you. It will take faith to believe it is possible, it will take courage to step out, and it will take commitment to see it through. Just remember: with God, nothing is impossible!

—Barbie Armenta

Be strong and courageous, and do the work. Do not be afraid
or discouraged, for the Lord God, my God, is with you.
—1 Chronicles 28:20

PART 1

TWO LIVES . . . ONE SPARK

CHAPTER 1

Richard and Barbie Yahoo!

Finding Hope After Divorce

I just don't want this night to end.
—Richard

"PADLOCK LOOKING FOR THE RIGHT COMBINATION."

That was the first line of Richard's Yahoo! Personals dating profile the day he reached out to me about getting together to meet.

Hmm. I like it!

After a while, it seems like you've seen and heard it all. I'd had my hopes of meeting the right guy crushed more than once, so I had recently decided to take a break from the online dating scene. Yet there I was again, scrolling through my potential matches, feeling more than a little bit panicked as a week of lonely days stretched ahead of me. My kids were scheduled to visit their dad for spring break, and as much as I didn't want to admit it, I just couldn't stand the thought of being alone. A seven-day free trial on Yahoo! Personals was all the encouragement I needed to get back in the game and give it one more chance.

I had only been back online a few hours when the note came: "I have no idea where Aubrey, Texas is, but maybe we should meet."

Not exactly the strongest start, but I was intrigued. I scrolled through Richard's profile trying to get a feel for the guy before making the leap.

He is cute!

He had uploaded a few pictures with friends and family and a couple more with his beautiful daughter. In my head, I was running down the list of positives and checking them off enthusiastically. His profile read like someone who knew how to have fun, but the part that finally got my attention was that he was a Christian. I so wanted to meet someone who could walk with me as I grew in my faith.

What do I have to lose? I typed back an answer, and he responded right away: "Let's meet somewhere in the middle. How about Sherlock's in Addison? Friday for happy hour? 4?"

I was feeling a little excited. This guy looked promising, but I was still nervous. I'd had too many bad first dates, so I agreed to meet him with a full backup plan in place in the event that the date went south. I had reached out to my girlfriends just in case I wanted to meet up with them later.

Maybe past experience was clouding my ability to keep a positive focus. Whatever it was, I did not give it 100 percent. I didn't even dress my cutest. There I was, waiting outside of Sherlock's at 4:00 p.m. wearing an outfit that was slightly nicer than casual—jeans, heels, and a white eyelet top (which he later told me reminded him of something his sisters would wear when they were little), but as soon as I saw him, I let out a sigh of regret. I knew I'd made a mistake. I should have worn my best outfit for sure.

He's Gorgeous

Richard is Puerto Rican, so I noticed his beautiful, tan skin and thick, dark hair right away. The pictures on his profile were encouraging, but in person, holy moly. He was almost too good to be true—classic tall, dark, and handsome good looks. He had a great smile. He obviously worked out. His arms were fantastic, and his body was lean and toned. And then, jackpot! I noticed he was wearing jeans with flip-flops, and I was all in on seeing where this date would take me. Check, check, check! I had never felt that kind of instant attraction to anyone. It was like lightning struck—and then I was suddenly very nervous.

I hope he calls again. Why did I wear this shirt? Richard was telling me about himself, but my head was spinning with all these crazy thoughts and questions. I was completely taken by his easygoing manner, and I loved every minute we spent talking and getting to know each other. I especially loved how full of life he was—he talked loud and laughed even louder. There was a joy in his spirit that was just amazing, and I was drawn in by his charm and wit. I wanted to know more about this man. I was glad I had given this online dating thing one last shot, and I was hoping that Richard felt the same. At some point, we realized that we didn't even know each other's last name. I asked him for his and pulled out my phone to change his contact information. I showed him how I had him listed in my phone—Richard Yahoo. He smiled and held up his phone for me to see. There I was—Barbie Yahoo. I, of course, thought it was a sign.

When we got ready to leave the restaurant, Richard said he wasn't ready for the night to end. "Let's go dancing," he said. I was thrilled. Dancing sounded like so much fun. I had raised my eyebrows and looked down at the flip-flops on his feet as we left. He laughed and assured me that he had real shoes stashed in the car. I guess you never know when you'll want to dance.

Richard is an amazing dancer. He attracted a lot of attention from other women on the dance floor, but that night I felt all of his focus on me. I went with the flow and danced wherever Richard wanted to dance. He was so much fun, and he kinda got me out of my shell. I liked it. We danced to everything from Flo Rida's "Apple Bottom Jeans" to a throw-back of the Sugar Hill Gang's "Rapper's Delight." We ended the night with Bob Marley's "No, Woman, No Cry." It was one of the best nights I'd had in a long time. You know that thing guys do when you're dancing, and they hold your hand against their chest? Yes, he did that. He was already stealing my heart.

You have to love a man who knows how to lead on a dance floor. It made me optimistic for how he would lead in life. I was probably putting the cart before the horse, but I couldn't help feeling this was just perfect. When I had gotten divorced three years earlier, I had lost hope that God could still have an amazing relationship for me. That night was the first time I had ever had a date like that. It gave me a glimpse of what was possible and renewed my hope.

And it was far from over. I could not have been more excited when Richard asked if I wanted to go for pancakes. I am not sure I had ever had that much fun on a date. We talked over pancakes until almost 4:00 a.m. The place was crowded and very noisy, but Richard had all my attention. I barely remember noticing anything that was going on around us or if I even ate. I listened to every word of every story Richard told. We covered a lot of ground, sharing about our past, and basically broke all of the dating "rules." I appreciate someone who doesn't play all of the dating games and can have real conversation. When we got ready to leave, he walked me to my car and kissed me good night in the parking lot. That night was even more fabulous than I hoped it would be!

Date Two

Since my kids were still with their dad, I was excited that Richard agreed to come over for dinner the next night. I was so proud of the home I had recently purchased for my boys and myself. It was a little—well, maybe a lot—out of the way, but the location made it affordable, and I loved its fabulous southern style and the front porch swing. Living in that little community was an escape for me from my old life. It was my safe place, and it allowed me to feel like I was doing right by my boys. The divorce had changed our lifestyle drastically, and moving there felt like we had made a step back up.

I didn't usually invite men over to my house, but that time I felt like I could make an exception. I really liked Richard, so I made one of my Italian favorites, Chicken Marbella with angel hair pasta, I hoped he would be impressed with my "domestic skills." When he arrived at my house, he was as good looking as I remembered. We spent a few minutes in my favorite place, my front porch swing, and we picked up where we had left off the night before, chatting over a glass of wine. I still had butterflies.

Richard and I enjoyed a delicious dinner and another glass of wine. It was always a plus when I don't burn anything! (I love to cook, but things don't always go as planned.) We were enjoying another really great night together. We talked some more, and he helped me clear the dishes from the table before we moved to the living room to relax on the couch. We kissed, and it was fireworks. There was no mistaking the chemistry between us. Then it happened. Richard stopped kissing me and said, "Can we not have sex? It's just been a long time."

In my head, I was okay with him wanting to slow down. That was kind of sweet, right? We kissed a couple more times, but Richard stopped again and told me maybe it was time for him to leave. *Why?* I didn't really get it. I was so not prepared for what he was about to say. That gorgeous man told me that he had made a commitment to himself and to God that he would no longer have sex outside of marriage.

Really?

Thoughts raced through my head. *It's not like we're eighteen. Who are we fooling? We've both been married before.* Richard left me stunned and a little panicked. I totally would have had sex with him that night. I wondered if he knew that. I wondered if I had blown it with him. If there was anything to wonder, it was flying through my head since I have always been a bit of an overthinker. That was all not on my radar, but I had to gather my thoughts and sort through them later. In spite of my walk to be a better Christian, I had never considered this aspect of dating. Is it really possible for someone to date this way after divorce, or was Richard just not interested in me?

The next morning, I had to call him to see where I stood. He was a gentleman and so nice. He reassured me that he'd had a great time and that he was looking forward to getting to know me better. I was relieved and maybe just a little bit sad. I knew this was a good thing, but it was just so foreign.

The next day, as I was sharing with my girlfriend about my two dates with Richard, she laughed because it sounded like something from a romantic comedy. I knew it all sounded crazy and too good to be true, but it really happened, and it gave me a hope that I had not felt in a long time.

> *I met the most amazing man this week! His name is Richard. He is completely different from any man I have ever met. He has a larger-than-life personality. He is incredibly handsome and has a huge heart for the Lord. Our first date we totally clicked. We talked, we laughed, and we danced. It was so perfect! Please God, I hope so much that this is for real.*
> —Barbie's Journal

FINDING YOUR RIGHT COMBINATION

What Barbie Learned About Finding Hope After Divorce

When we find ourselves single again, most of us just focus on filling the empty space that's left behind. We lose our identity; our self-esteem takes a blow; we're lost. We don't know how to move forward alone, so we repeat our comfortable patterns, expecting that the next relationship will somehow be different. When it isn't, we find ourselves reliving those old feelings of guilt and shame—feeling worthless and right where Satan wants us. When my marriage ended, I lost hope. Hope that God could still have a beautiful relationship for me.

What I realized is that I was putting my hope in the wrong place. I was putting my hope in a man and not God. We cannot put God expectations on a man; they will fail us every time. God's Word says that he has an abundant life for us. It does not say, unless we get divorced. God's grace covers it all. You are worthy. He gives us the thrill of hope.

What God's Word Says About Finding Hope

Blessed are those whose help is the God of Jacob, whose hope is in the LORD their God. (Psalm 146:5)

"For I know the plans I have for you," declares the LORD, "plans to prosper you and not to harm you, plans to give you hope and a future." (Jeremiah 29:11)

May the God of hope fill you with all joy and peace as you trust in him, so that you may overflow with hope by the power of the Holy Spirit. (Romans 15:13)

"My grace is sufficient for you, for my power is made perfect in weakness." Therefore I will boast all the more gladly about my weaknesses, so that Christ's power may rest on me. (2 Corinthians 12:9)

Now faith is confidence in what we hope for and assurance about what we do not see. (Hebrews 11:1)

As God shows you more Scriptures that relate to finding hope, write them on this page too.

☙❦❧

Isaiah 40:31; Romans 8:23–25; Philippians 1:6; Colossians 1:27; 1 Peter 5:10

Begin Your Own Process

- In what ways have you lost hope?
- What are you hoping for in your future?
- What would it mean to you to receive what you are hoping for?

As you go through the chapters, spend some time in prayer before you work through "Begin Your Own Process." Ask God what he wants to show you in your own life. Let him show you patterns that you need to let go of and give you the courage to move forward.

CHAPTER 2

Where It All Began: Richard (Part 1)

Bondage and Freedom

I want to be better, but I don't know what better looks like. I want to see myself the way God sees me.
—Richard

EVERY STORY HAS A BEGINNING, and in many ways, I often feel that my journey with Barbie began with one simple decision to obey God and walk through life honoring his laws and direction as I understand the Bible. When I look back, I clearly see how that one choice touched and changed not only my life but also her life, our kids' lives, and possibly the lives of others I will never know.

Arriving at that decision was a rocky road—to be honest, nearly a rock-bottom road. I came really close to hitting the bottom, maybe more than once, before I was willing to hear and embrace God's call on my life. It was never for lack of effort on his part. From an early age, I was aware that he was tapping me on the shoulder. But hey, guys like me didn't really do the God thing. So I was always kind of tossing a hand up to say, "Yeah, I hear you, but I'm busy now. Let's do this another time, okay?"

When I was in my mid-thirties, he began to tap a little harder, and I have some clear memories of times when I absolutely cannot deny hearing his voice or perceiving his presence.

I remember one particular night during a friend's visit. He and I were set for a big night on the town, which usually meant a big party at the Dallas nightclubs. We'd drink and get our dance on with all the prettiest single girls in the metroplex, and if everything went according to plan, well, there'd be a little bonus at the end of the night. I'm not proud of it, but that was life at the time.

We were in the car with the music turned up so loud you could feel the beat of the bass rumble through the speakers. Speeding down I-30, we joked and laughed and caught up about all that was happening in our hometown. If the mood struck us, we'd bust out and sing along with a favorite song. We were both looking forward to a great weekend.

My weekends had become the best part of my life since my divorce three years earlier. My favorite times were when my daughter was with me for the weekend, but when I faced time alone, I filled in the empty space by going out to let loose and have a little fun. Whichever way I spent them, these were the only times I escaped the constant stress of making ends meet and battling all that comes with a difficult divorce. Time had not eased the friction, and I had begun to believe the voices in my head pointing out all the ways I was a failure as a husband and a father. Even outside the marriage, I felt the blows of discontent wearing me down. I don't think I was completely aware of how close I was to breaking down, but on some level I sensed it. It took all the energy I had to put on my happy face and hide the fact that I was unraveling, but I was going to hide it at any cost. I knew I'd figure it out; I always had.

Anyway, my buddy and I were headed out for our night on the town when I got the weirdest feeling—a familiar, almost creepy sense that we weren't alone. I'd felt it before. It was like feeling the hairs on your neck rise when someone is watching you. I could almost feel the presence of someone in the car with us. I tried to smooth over it and ignore it, but it persisted until finally I reached up, flipped the volume down on the radio, and looked over at my friend. Why I felt the need to announce what was going on inside me is a complete mystery, but I did it anyway.

"Dude," I said, "I feel like God is sitting in the back seat right behind me, tapping on my shoulder. It's like he's got his arms wide open, and he's asking me, 'When are you coming home?' Is that weird or what?"

I don't know what I was thinking he might say. I was coming out of left field, for sure. I waited until he finally looked over at me with this kind of blank, what-are-you-talking-about expression. The silence dangled between us, uncomfortably long. Finally he raised a questioning brow.

"Yep," he responded, drawing out his words for effect. "That. Is. Definitely. Weird!"

I couldn't help but let out a big laugh, so we both gave in to the moment to glide over the awkwardness of it, and as quickly as it had come over me, the feeling disappeared. Shrugging, I reached out, turned up the tunes, and erased the incident from my thoughts for the moment. I wasn't about to let anything get in the way of our having a great time that night.

From Living for Myself to Dadhood

I've always loved a good time. It's who I am and what I do, and I guess my story started there. I was the life of the party, the fearless, happy-go-lucky, big-smile, big-laugh guy, always happy and game for just about anything anyone threw at me. I had no fear, and my friends always said they loved going out with me because I made things happen. I wanted to squeeze every bit of fun out of life that I could. I guess I was like a lot of guys out there. I believed I was invincible and that I'd never get caught up in anything I couldn't handle. At the end of the day, I believed I was a good guy, but I was, for sure, all about me—never gave a thought to what my choices might be dumping into someone else's life.

At a very early age, I had a sexual curiosity that was way beyond my years, and by the time I was in high school, I was dating girls much older than myself. I grew up in the fast lane—I drank, stayed out too late, and had lots of sex—and I didn't have any reason to slow down as I got older.

By the time graduation happened, I was ready to get on with my life as soon as I could get a job. So of course my living-on-the-edge attitude had me packed up and moved in with my twenty-five-year-old girlfriend before my parents knew what happened. They were ticked at me over that one, but as far as I was concerned they didn't have a say.

Within a few months, I had talked my girlfriend into sharing a new place with a good friend and his girlfriend. On our own, young and fresh, we were ready to let the good times roll. Looking back, it was like I opened Pandora's box with that one simple decision. It wasn't long before one of my girlfriend's good friends introduced me and my friends to recreational drugs—mostly snorting speed—and we started on a whole new path that quickly became a routine part of my life. I was living large and having a great time doing what I wanted when I wanted. I thought I was just a guy having fun—no strings attached.

Eventually my girlfriend and I broke up. Around the same time, my job changed, and I moved away from my hometown. I looked forward to new adventures and new people, so moving promised to be another fun time. I was easygoing and made friends easily, so I didn't worry about starting over somewhere new. Life was one big party, and I was having a great time in spite of the occasional wakeup calls that were probably meant to get me on track. Honestly, I don't know how I didn't get caught up in some pretty serious consequences when I think back on those days.

I should have known that my willingness to constantly test the limits would catch up with me, and I'd have to pay the piper. On the rare occasion when something bad was about to happen, I'd sometimes tell myself to get it together. But when the fuss died down, those thoughts would quickly go away.

I never lacked confidence when it came to girls. I dated a lot and had more than my share of hookups. The problem is, when you play with fire, sometimes you or someone else gets burned—sometimes both of you. I found this out the hard way in my late twenties, right before I moved to

Dallas. One of the girls I had been seeing ended up pregnant. It had not been a serious relationship, at least not for me, and there was no way I was ready to settle down to be a husband or a dad. I was honest with her, and I think it put her in a bad spot. She was still young, and she couldn't take care of a kid on her own, so our relationship ended kind of ugly when we decided she should get an abortion. I told myself I wasn't in love, and I couldn't see how it might ever work out anyway. Over time, I had plenty of other reasons that justified our choice. I moved on and learned to deal with any doubts that hung around in the back of my mind. But the decision to abort a child stays with you forever.

Never wanting to find myself in that position again, I took more precautions against another pregnancy. But even using protection, it wasn't long until I found myself faced with the same decision. New girl, same circumstance. But this time something made me pause.

I wasn't any more prepared for the news the second time than I had been the first. *What do I do? Do I marry this person I hardly know? Do I leave her to handle it on her own?* This time, like the first, I wasn't in love, and I sure as heck wasn't responsible enough to be a dad. I was barely responsible enough to take care of myself, much less a wife and a kid. Nonetheless, I couldn't shake the feeling that I wasn't supposed to just turn my back. I cared a little more this time. Maybe the lingering guilt from the last time made me stop to reconsider my choices.

The timing and circumstances weren't perfect for becoming parents for me or the woman I was seeing. We barely knew each other, but we both came to the same conclusion—we wanted to do the right thing and go through with the pregnancy. I remember telling her that I couldn't promise her a Cinderella, fairy-tale ending, but I could promise to give it all I had to be a good dad to my kid. It was all that I was capable of at the time, so we moved in together and stumbled our way through the next few months.

In spite of our good intentions to be responsible, loving parents to our baby, neither of us was in love. We decided to give it some time before jumping into any big commitments and settled on testing the waters together as a couple as we waited on our daughter to arrive. We eventually grew to care for each other, but we struggled every day for more than that.

My daughter, Daylee, was born the following July, and man, there's nothing like a baby to open up a guy's heart. Holding her in my arms, I think I fell in love for the first time in my life. Nothing I'd ever known compared to the feelings I had for her. At the same time, nothing compared to the fear that gripped me when the reality settled in that I would be responsible for her. Like so much of my life up to that point, I see-sawed with the pull of the good and bad of it all, but more than anything, she made me want to be more than I was. She made me want to be a better man and a good father.

As for her mother and me, we just kept trying to figure it out. When Daylee was born, we still weren't in love, but we'd fallen into a comfortable zone that, in the end, gave us the courage to try to give our daughter the opportunity to grow up in a loving family. We decided to get married when she was about a year old.

I wish I could say we had a happy ending. As well as any two people can, we tried to find our way as a couple and as parents, but it was an uphill battle. I made my first serious efforts to be a stand-up guy. I gave up my old partying habits, worked harder at my job, was faithful to my wife, and started attending church—everything and more that I'd seen my parents do for me and my brothers and sisters as a kid. For both my wife and me, this was completely new territory that challenged us to move outside of our selfishness and stretched us into uncomfortable territories of self-sacrifice and giving.

Fatherhood was an especially hard time for me as I attempted to adjust my previous definitions of myself to fit the new roles I'd assumed. I worked hard to measure up to what I thought I should be, but I often felt that I fell short in the eyes of my wife. As time wore on, we began to argue more, and I grew less interested in making the efforts that I knew would make her happy. At the end of every argumentative encounter, I would ask myself what I was still doing in the relationship. It seemed that nothing I did or said was ever good enough.

I don't think either of us had our hearts "all in" when it came to doing the real work needed to iron out our differences, and going through the motions was not enough to strengthen a marriage that was already built on a rocky foundation. Within three years of our beginning, we came to our end.

Torn by Anger

When my wife filed for divorce, for the first time I could recall, I felt the wheels coming off and my life beginning to spin out of control.

Her announcement to divorce me came closely on the heels of my dad's death three months earlier. I was still reeling from that loss, and even though we'd been on shaky ground, I had always believed there was something I could do to make our marriage better. So when I was served with the divorce papers, I felt like I'd been sucker punched.

Whatever great strides I felt I had gained in my life and with God were suddenly shattered. I became angry at God, life, and all the people who I felt had betrayed me. That anger would be my weakness; as I crumbled under the weight of the stress, it sent me tailspinning into some pretty dark places over the next few years.

Following our separation, I moved out of our house into a small apartment that left a lot to be desired. I became more and more angry with the world. I resented that I had lost my wife, my daughter, and my dad all at the same time. In my mind, I'd been working so hard to do the right thing, and now I was confused and hurt. I believed I had been making all the right choices. *And this is what I get? Thanks, but if that's what a loving God does, I'll pass.*

It didn't help that my ex-wife was moving on with another relationship. Like a little boy crying, "No fair!" I couldn't get past the bitterness that she was somehow being rewarded while I stood by with nothing. I couldn't understand why my life had tanked so badly. *How could all my efforts end up in a heap of nothing?*

I found myself living with so much emotional pain, and rejection and loss hung over me every day. The voice telling me I wasn't good enough grew louder and louder until I started to believe it was truth. It was then that the temptation of old patterns rose up and threatened to suck me back into comfortable arms.

The hardest part of the divorce was the emptiness of living most of my days without my little girl. It was unbearable to have her taken from being such a big part of my daily life to being scheduled into a couple of days every other weekend and predetermined holidays. It seemed wrong that dads got so little time with their kids when a marriage ended, but I didn't have the money to involve myself in a custody fight. Besides, I just didn't want to do that to my daughter. At four, she deserved better than to be the center of such a drama.

Eventually the news came that my ex would be remarrying, and that meant further complications for me and Daylee. My daughter would see another man more often than she saw me, and I felt threatened— afraid that he could become more of a father to her than I would have the opportunity to be. *Would she call him Dad too?* The threat of losing my little girl whom I cherished clouded my reason, and I struggled to stay on steady ground. I found it hard not to feel betrayed—by God and by everyone I knew.

In the midst of the stress, my old comfort zones offered relief, and it didn't take me long to fall back into them. Even though I continued attending church, I wasn't strong enough in my walk with Christ to weather the storm around me, and I wasn't surrounding myself with friends who were living for Christ or providing me with examples of better ways to become the man I wanted to be. I didn't know how to surrender myself and my troubles to God's care.

So I gravitated back to familiar friends and behaviors to cope with my losses and dull the pain. Unfortunately, I found myself ramping up with increasingly risky behaviors. I had snorted meth in the past, but new friends introduced me to smoking it in the months following my separation and divorce. I loved the intense, quick high of smoking it, and I started using it more and more often to dull the ache. I never gave a thought to the price I might pay for welcoming it into my life.

I'd always believed I had control over my drug use, and maybe I did at one point. But once I started smoking meth, it became clear that I was no longer deciding when I would use. What I had always done for fun in the past quickly spiraled into a habit. Smoking was way more effective at making me feel like the old me, but I was falling to pieces and denying it the whole way.

Bound by Bad Choices

Apart from my weekends with my daughter, I slid quietly into a hopeless place and began taking chances I'd never taken before, defiantly content to do what I wanted, how I wanted, when I wanted. I forgot to pay rent or bills. I let the little details slip through the cracks—ignoring parking tickets, refusing to make good on a bad check, showing up at work a little late, failing to get my daughter where she needed to be on time. None of it seemed like a big deal. I made excuses and justified all my mistakes. I mean, I always took care of my business sooner or later, right?

Weekends were my Jekyll-and-Hyde times. On alternating weekends, I played mom and dad to my young daughter, trying hard to do and be everything she needed while hiding the guy I was the rest of the time from her and my ex. The off weekends were my time for letting out a breath. I'd spend Friday and Saturday nights clubbing, drinking, smoking meth, and having sex.

My little mistakes soon started turning into bigger ones. I was taking more risks without considering how my choices could impact my daughter. Coming home to my apartment one night after picking her up for the weekend, I walked up the breezeway and turned the corner to the staircase leading up to my apartment only to discover a lock handle on the doorknob. My heart sank. I had been locked out for not paying my rent that month. The embarrassment and anxiety staggered me. I needed to come up with a plan immediately, before Daylee noticed that anything was wrong; the last thing I needed was for my ex to get wind of it. So I told Daylee that we were going to play a game. I asked her to wait for me on the stairs below while I went up and broke into my own place.

That wouldn't be the last time I escaped a mishap while she was in my care. Another incident that really shook me up was when I barely escaped arrest on an outstanding warrant for a bad check while Daylee was riding with me in the car. I was finally beginning to understand that I needed to pull myself together—if not for myself, then for her. I knew I needed to redirect before I ended up in real trouble.

As crazy as it sounds, and in spite of my anger with God, I never stopped attending church through all the chaos. No matter what I did on Friday and Saturday, I could be found in the rear of the sanctuary at Fellowship Church in Grapevine, Texas, every Sunday morning. I never missed a service. Week after week, I came alone and full of misgiving. In my heart I knew that I wasn't living my life the way I should be, but I just couldn't figure out how to do it differently. There wasn't one sermon preached where I didn't walk away feeling as if the pastor was reading my emails or text messages. I would ask myself, *How does he know?* It was like he was talking directly to me, like he had a window into my world.

Most times I would just sit with tears streaming down my cheeks, asking myself what I was doing with my life. I was completely ashamed of the way I was living, but I was unwilling to give up on the choices I was making. Driven by my resentment, I put tremendous energy into fighting what I knew was right. I felt cheated, and the anger I harbored, which had become my captor, left me feeling conflicted—comfortable and uncomfortable, both at the same time.

FINDING YOUR RIGHT COMBINATION

What Richard Learned About Freedom and Bondage

Richard, like many of us, wasn't in literal physical bondage. He lived in an emotional and spiritual bondage of his own making. These are the things that can keep you too from moving forward in life.

Bad decisions, wrong relationships, addiction—despite the fact that he had a beautiful daughter and had found a church that he loved, Richard continued to let his internal battles of anger, insecurity, and unworthiness keep him stuck. Richard turned to drugs, partying, and women to fill what only God could fill. And all of them left him empty—because true freedom comes only from God.

God was shining a light on the areas of Richard's life that weren't working. But it took some time before he made real change.

What God's Word Says About Freedom and Bondage

Jesus replied, "I tell you the truth, everyone who sins is a slave of sin." (John 8:34 NLT)

We must obey God rather than human beings! (Acts 5:29)

I want to do what is good, but I don't. I don't want to do what is wrong, but I do it anyway. (Romans 7:19 NLT)

So Christ has truly set us free. Now make sure that you stay free, and don't get tied up again in slavery to the law. (Galatians 5:1 NLT)

They promise freedom, but they themselves are slaves of sin and corruption. For you are a slave to whatever controls you. (2 Peter 2:19 NLT)

As God shows you more Scriptures that relate to freedom and bondage, write them on this page too.

⊙

Psalm 119:45; 1 Corinthians 6:12; 2 Corinthians 3:17;
Galatians 5:13–14; Ephesians 3:12

Begin Your Own Process

- Are there any areas of your life where you are in bondage?
- What do you turn to for comfort?
- It's said that we become like the five people we hang around the most. Take a few minutes to take an inventory of the people in your life. Are there any relationships you might need to distance yourself from? This might even include "unfriending" on social media. What we see while scrolling can influence us in many ways.

Remember that freedom is not just the absence of something; it is also the presence of Someone. Our most important relationship is with God.

CHAPTER 3

Where It All Began: Barbie

Relationships with God and People

If you want to walk on water, you've got to get out of the boat.
—John Ortberg

I NEVER IN A MILLION YEARS would have thought I'd find myself abandoning my home with my three sons in the middle of the Christmas holiday. Yet there I was one December day, phone pressed between my shoulder and my ear, as I reached out to my best friend Tracey for support.

"I think I'm packing," I said, when she answered the phone.

"It's about time!" she responded.

Only two nights before, I had called her at 2:00 a.m. and attempted to tell her, through tears, about another fight I'd had with my husband. She was so great to listen, even when she could barely understand me. Unfortunately, this was a familiar call, and she knew exactly what I was trying to say. Only this time it felt different. Maybe I would actually do something about it.

It was a Saturday morning two weeks before Christmas, and I found myself walking through the house carrying a medium-size box in my arms. I don't even remember where I got the box. One minute I was holding my breath, and the next I was mindlessly wandering from room to room through our home. I picked random things from the shelves and counters and gazed at them blankly, hoping I would magically know if I needed to put the items in the box or leave them behind. With no clear direction, I continued through the rooms adding items that someone might take in a fire, like baby books and my kids' photographs.

I had been married for twelve years, and that morning I found myself preparing to leave my husband and our home. Like most women who find themselves in an abusive relationship, I had not planned ahead. I just knew that it was now or never.

I was heartbroken that I was once again leaving a marriage. The reasons I was leaving this time weren't the same as in my previous marriage, but here I was again. I couldn't understand how I could make another mistake. My parents have been married forever, and I always thought that would be me too. I never thought I would be divorced once, much less twice. All I'd ever wanted was to be a good wife and mother and live a normal suburban life. I wondered why I couldn't make things work. What would this do to my kids? I still lived in denial, believing that they might not even be aware their dad and I were struggling. I thought I was hiding my fear and emotional pain, taking the verbal blows to save them so that they could have a "good life."

Deciding to leave wasn't easy. We had attended marriage counseling and a marriage retreat, I was reading books and my Bible, but nothing seemed to help. I struggled knowing that Scripture says things like God hates divorce and that I am to submit to my husband. No matter what we did, we couldn't escape the never-ending cycle of drama.

When things were good, I walked on eggshells in an attempt to preserve the peace—keeping the house picked up, the kids' toys out of the driveway, and the meals cooked. I avoided behaviors that might make him angry and put him over the edge. It didn't matter. I felt I could never be good enough to meet his expectations. I was careful to try to hide our fights, which more often than not, took place under the cover of night when the boys were asleep. At least I hoped they were asleep. The light of day would bring apologies, a card, or maybe a make-up lunch, and we would reenter a "honeymoon period" where I would hold out hope that things might get better for good this time. I prayed and I begged God for things to change, but nothing ever did. I was exhausted and ashamed, and I was finally beginning to understand that I had a greater responsibility to protect my boys.

Two days earlier, I had found myself sitting on the floor of my living room at 2:00 a.m. The Christmas tree lay on the floor following another fit of temper that ended in my husband knocking it to the ground. Pieces of broken ornaments lay all over the floor, and I sat gathering them up and trying to save any that might have escaped unharmed. I wanted to undo as much of the damage as possible before the boys woke in the morning. I could easily explain away the broken ornaments as an unfortunate accident, but the truth made my heart sink.

The action seemed intentionally aimed at taking away something I couldn't replace. Our Christmas tree was loaded with special ornaments, reflections of moments frozen in time: Nate played soccer one year. Michael played football. Dalton loved the movie *Monsters, Inc.* I sat there with tears in my eyes looking at their shattered memories on the floor before letting my gaze trail around the room and finally land on a holiday sign sitting on my fireplace mantel. HOPE was spelled out in large, shiny, silver letters. In that moment, I realized I had lost mine. I knew I had been deceiving myself, and I suddenly had a picture in my mind that I was not doing what was best for my boys. Something had to change. And that's how I found myself alone that Saturday morning, wandering the house with my box of treasures.

Our city's high school football team was playing in the Texas state high school football championship that afternoon. My husband had taken the boys to the game earlier that morning, and I stayed behind to finish up last-minute Christmas preparation. He left the house yelling at me on his way to the back door, and my stomach knotted in familiar anxiety. Usually after a night of outbursts, we would have a time of calm and apologies. It was unusual for his mood to be this bad so soon.

I had sighed with relief at the sound of the closing door. I relaxed a little knowing I could let my guard down for a while. As if on autopilot, I made my way to our study and sat down at the computer. As I had done many times before, I googled the descriptions for verbal and emotional abuse. I didn't do it so much to prove that I was abused as to prove that I wasn't. Never in my wildest dreams did I ever think this could happen to me. I did not want to see myself as a victim. *How did I get here?*

Without warning, my husband suddenly rushed in through the front door right next to the study. He yelled out in a continuation of his previous tirade, and I was frozen in place. My heart raced. I was terrified that he would see what I was reading and that his anger would push over the top. I quickly exited out of the screen and sat quietly at the desk as he tore through the house in search of something forgotten. He finally left again, slamming the door so hard the windows shook. For a brief moment, I almost opened the screen on the computer again, but I realized I didn't need to prove anything. The truth was crystal clear.

Making the Break

The next thing I remember was walking through the house with the box in one hand and my phone in the other as I called Tracey to see if the boys and I could stay at her house for a few days until I figured out what I was going to do. I was so grateful for an incredible friend who faithfully stood by me in my mess. I talked with her as I finished collecting the few things we might need, and I loaded up my car with our clothes and my box. I drove in disbelief to Tracey's house, where I dropped off our things before returning to my house to wait for the boys' return.

I don't know how long I waited for them. Time seemed to stand still as I stood looking out my kitchen window with a lump in my throat and my heart pounding. When I finally saw the white car pull in the drive, I gathered the courage I would need to get us out the door. My goal was simple. All I wanted was to get myself and the boys out of the house without my husband knowing what I was up to and without another fight.

The boys burst loudly into the house, talking all at once, filling me in on the details of the big game and assuring me that I was sorry I missed it. And, just like it was any other Saturday, I invited them to come along to the grocery store. I knew they would want to go because they were always up for running errands with me. I casually called out to my husband that we were leaving for the store, piled the boys into the car, and headed for the unknown. Once we were safely at Tracey's, I called my husband to let him know that we would not be returning home.

I had no idea what we were going to do next.

I felt homeless but not hopeless.
—Barbie

The next couple of weeks were an emotional roller coaster. I left on a Saturday, and by Sunday afternoon I was already doubting my decision and wondering if I should go back. *What was I thinking? How will I take care of my boys? Am I doing the right thing to take them away from their dad?* In spite of the doubts that filled my mind, I held firm, supported all the way by Tracey and my family. (I have since heard that women go back to an abusive home an average of seven times.)

Of course he had been angry when I called, and he assumed that I had been planning to leave for some time. There was nothing I could say at that point to convince him otherwise. He decided to visit his family in Amarillo, Texas.

The next day, the boys and I met my mom for lunch. As I told her what was happening, I began to panic about our future. I told her that maybe I should follow him to Amarillo and talk to him, thinking it might be different but knowing in my heart that it wouldn't. That day there was a huge snowstorm that closed the roads between Dallas and Amarillo. Thankfully, I couldn't have gone to him if I'd really wanted to. I now see that snowstorm as God's protection.

My boys and I spent the next two weeks living with Tracey, then with my sister and her family, and I soon filed for divorce. A friend from church was helpful in getting my husband to allow the boys and me to move back into our house while we waited for it to sell. It was good for the kids to be in their home. I feared their dad might show up unexpectedly, but he never did.

I began the slow process of building a new life, but I worried constantly about how I would keep us afloat financially. A few years prior, a girlfriend and I had purchased a franchise. And like most entrepreneurs in the early stages of a business, I wasn't sure we were going to be able to survive on my income.

The boys fell into a rhythm of visits with their dad, and I did my best to stay out of the line of fire. I didn't want to stand in the way of any relationship they had with their dad, but I couldn't try to be friends with him either. More than anything, I knew I needed to heal emotionally and to take a hard look at myself before I could move forward, either alone or in another relationship. It was easy to want to blame our failed marriage on my husband, but I also needed to understand how I had contributed to the breakdown. This was my second divorce, and there was no denying that the common denominator was me. Owning my responsibility was one of the hardest things I'd ever done, but accepting it opened up a door to something better than I could have ever dreamed up on my own. I was trusting God like I never had before to get me and my boys to a better place, and it was becoming clearer every day that he was working in our lives.

A few years before my divorce, I had received an invitation to a prayer night from one of the wives of my husband's business associates. I hadn't grown up in church, so attending her gathering was outside my comfort zone. The only thing I knew about her at the time was that she was a "Mary Kay Lady." Honestly, I wasn't sure I wanted Mary Kay products any more than I wanted prayer, but with three young boys at home, the thought of getting out of the house for some adult time was all the encouragement I needed to accept her invitation.

When I arrived at Sue's house, I felt welcome immediately. She was about my age, with cute, short brown hair (and great makeup, of course). The first thing she said to me was that I was pretty, a coveted word to a woman who had given birth to three kids and didn't hear it often.

She took me inside and introduced me to the other women who were there. I noticed they were all so nice and seemed so happy.

We gathered for the prayer time after visiting, and I moved to the back, nervously hoping no one would ask me to talk. I wasn't ready for anyone to know that I didn't have a clue what they were discussing. So I listened, mesmerized by a woman who shared from the book *If You Want to Walk on Water, You've Got to Get Out of the Boat* by John Ortberg, and who recounted the Bible story from Matthew 14:22–32 of Peter walking on water to Jesus.

Jesus's disciples were in a boat quite a distance from shore, when the wind and waves really picked up. Jesus walked on the water out to the boat. The disciples thought he was a ghost and were terrified. Jesus said, "Take courage! It is I. Don't be afraid." So Peter said, "Lord, if it's you, tell me to come to you on the water." "Come," he said. So Peter got out of the boat and began walking toward Jesus. But Peter got scared by the waves, took his focus off Jesus, and began sinking. "Lord, save me!" he cried. Jesus caught his hand, spoke to him, and walked back to the boat with him. When they climbed in, the winds died down (paraphrased from the New International Version).

I can't tell you what happened that night, but there was something about that story that brought the Bible to life and made me realize just how relevant it was to me. What I heard her say was that when we focus our attention on Jesus, we can accomplish anything. It is when we focus on the "storms" around us that we sink. That was it! I was hooked. This was all I talked about for the next few days to any of my girlfriends who would listen. I am so grateful for Sue and her willingness to invite me to her house and share God's love with me.

Prior to that night, I had no idea how much God loved me and cared about what happened in my life. I had accepted Christ in the fifth grade at a church I occasionally attended with my friend from down the street, but on this day, I learned what it meant to have a relationship with Jesus.

I began reading and studying the Bible, and I soon signed up for a nine-month "walk through the Bible" at the church we had been attending. I could not get enough, and I was overwhelmed by my new understanding of God's love. I was so grateful to have a pastor who was patient with my lack of knowledge and for a God who met me right where I was. Without my knowing, God was laying a foundation for me that day that would carry me through some pretty rough times ahead.

Single, Lonely . . . and Learning

By the third month of our separation, the house sold, and the boys and I moved into a duplex nearby. Every day I was in my Bible, clinging to God and his Word to get through the day. One verse that I often read was "Happy is he who has the God of Jacob for his help, whose hope is in the LORD his God" (Psalm 146:5 NKJV). It reminded me that my hope was not found in a man, but it was found in God.

Despite the fact that I was praying, journaling, and reading my Bible daily, I was lonely. Imperfect as it had been, my husband and I had built a home and a life. We lived by our best friends. All I could see was that my life as I knew it was over. Suddenly I felt like Peter must have felt that stormy night—adrift in my little boat, all alone. I had to be strong for my kids, keep my business going, and pretend I wasn't falling apart. But on the inside I was full of doubt and began to suffer anxiety attacks. My anxiety didn't seem to need a source. I would be going about my day and suddenly have feelings of impending doom.

I had tried desperately to find a Christian counselor who could help me, but since I had left so close to Christmas, I could not find anyone available. One day while driving, I saw a large sign that said "Christian Counseling." I immediately pulled in the parking lot to see if I could make an appointment—but the door was locked. *You have got to be kidding me!* I needed someone to talk to who didn't know me. I loved my friends, but I knew they would be too likely to take my side. I needed someone to give me perspective and tell me what to do. I'd never felt so lost or beaten down, and I couldn't afford to let my kids or myself down again.

A friend encouraged me to call The Women's Haven domestic violence counseling center. All I could think was that I wasn't a victim of domestic violence because my husband didn't hit me. But I wasn't sure I could wait much longer to talk to someone, so I called. A friendly woman answered the phone, and I shared with her that I wasn't being physically abused, so I wasn't sure they could help. She asked me some questions, and after a few minutes on the phone, she assured me I had made the right decision to reach out.

It was through Safe Haven that I finally connected with an amazing counselor. As much as I didn't want to accept it, she summed up the cycle of violence for me in only a few minutes during my first visit. I was crushed. After spending so much time on the computer trying to prove to myself that I wasn't in an abusive relationship, it took her no time to lay out all the facts to confirm that I was. She described the cycle I had lived in perfectly, and I was suddenly angry. *Victim?* That was a label I didn't like, and I steamed with new resentment toward my ex for giving it to me. *How does this happen? Was I that naive?* It was so hard when people I knew said things to me like, "I wouldn't have put up with that," or "I would have left a long time ago." *Was I that dumb?* My doctor would later tell me that abuse happens gradually, that women don't always see the signs on the front end, and the next thing they know, they are in too far and not sure how to get out.

My feelings of anxiety continued to mount as I tried to navigate our new life. Some of my toughest times were when my boys would spend weekends with their dad. I was overwhelmed with loneliness and struggled with filling my time. To make matters worse, my oldest son, Nate, decided to move to Las Vegas to live with his dad. It was hard for me not to take it personally, but in my head I understood. I knew this was a great time in his life for him to be with his dad. At fifteen, I felt this was an important time for his dad to teach him guy things. No matter how much this made sense in my head, the day he got on the plane was one of the worst days of my life.

I was working so hard to make ends meet in my business and at home that when I did have empty spaces, which wasn't often as a single mom, I was overwhelmed with a need to fill them. I wanted someone to share life with, but I was pretty sure I wasn't going to find him while just sitting at home.

I wasn't exactly sure what I should do to meet men, so I decided to try online dating. What did I have to lose? It seemed like an easy way to get back in the game, and it gave me the chance to filter out anyone who didn't interest me, or who had a problem with my faith or the fact I had three boys. I spelled this out up front in my profile.

I met a few nice guys whom I found interesting, went to some nice restaurants and a couple of concerts, and enjoyed the flirting that goes with meeting someone new. It didn't take me long to discover that having someone text me "Good morning, beautiful!" felt really good . . . at least for a little while. I'd check my phone and computer for texts and messages to boost me one more time.

My counselor referred to the compliments as "codependent crack." They felt good in the moment, but the feeling was fleeting and left me wanting more. At one point my counselor asked me, "Do you know that you are beautiful, even if no one tells you?" Sadly, my answer was no. I didn't know it at the time, and I was looking for a man to tell me what God had already told me in his Word. God had told me that I am wonderfully made. God had told me that he makes all things good. Why was that so hard to believe?

I continued my ridiculous pattern of dating for a while, choosing to do it the way I imagined everyone else did. My perception of the rules of dating was, it wasn't a matter of *if* you were going to have sex, but how many dates was appropriate *before* you had sex. Of course, I had standards. I'd have never had sex on the first date. But I was a divorced woman with three kids. It never occurred to me that I once again had a choice to save myself for the right person. In my mind, that ship had sailed.

I got pretty good at reading online dating profiles to speed the process of narrowing my list of prospects. There were the guys with a list of "don't wants" that were actually a recounting of all the things they didn't like about their ex-wives. Then there were all the guys that said they were looking for someone "outdoorsy" or insisted that their perfect mate "must work out" in spite of the fact that their profile pic looked like they hadn't seen the inside of a gym or a hiking trail in quite a while. If their profile pic was shirtless, I was out immediately.

As time went by with no Mr. Right on the horizon, I began to ask myself why it was that the lonelier I felt, the more willing I was to compromise my beliefs and standards. I wanted to avoid going home to a quiet house, so I would find myself going further than I had planned or than I should have. I convinced myself that these poor guys were just good guys who hadn't met the right girl yet, and I might be the best thing that could ever happen to them. I never once asked myself whether or not a particular man was good for me. I was sure I would be the one who would bring out the best in them, and having someone, anyone, want me felt good for a while. Until I got home. I recall sitting on my floor with a blanket over my head, my Bible in my hand, and my heart full of shame and guilt at what I'd been willing to compromise to feel wanted.

My big aha moment came a couple of years after my divorce. I began dating a guy I met at the gym. He was handsome, stood 6'8" tall, and had a great smile. He took me on the *best* first date. He did all the right things: brought flowers, wined and dined me, and ended the night with a great evening stroll listening to live music. What more could a girl want? He told me on the first date that he never dated anyone for more than five months, believing that it was the right amount of time to know if the relationship was a fit. I went all in, believing he could be "the one."

Over the next four months we went on many dates, but none like the first one. I held on in anticipation of a repeat of the magic of that first night, but it never came. We fell into a comfortable routine, and I made the mistake of thinking that if I slept with him, things might change. Subconsciously, I probably believed sex would make our relationship more committed, deeper than it was in reality. I continued to push down my doubts and ignore signs that he wasn't "all in" to justify my actions. Then, you guessed it, the week before the five-month mark arrived, he abruptly ended the relationship. In spite of his pronouncement on our first date and all the signs that followed, I was still hurt, blindsided, and devastated.

I am so grateful today for how that turned out. I had picked up right where I left off with both my ex-husbands, repeating negative patterns and giving myself up to anything I thought might make someone love and accept me. That almost-five-month relationship, if you can call it that, helped me see more clearly that we don't find our value horizontally.

It's getting clearer every day. I have been taking the wrong paths when I feel the unexpected despair wash over me. I try to mask everything instead of working through it. I have to learn to feel. I have to allow myself to work through the pain. Having a date, phone call, or email is not going to heal me.
—Barbie's Journal

I was learning to turn to God, learning that my value came from God alone. My value was and is found in my vertical relationship with God. This lesson was preparing me for what was to come.

Another spring break was nearing, and I knew I was going to have a quiet week while the boys were at their dad's house.

One day I received an email advertising a seven-day free trial with Yahoo! Personals. "Well," I thought, "maybe I can find something to do this week." I signed up, and as I scrolled through the pics, I found a guy who was kind of cute and decided to contact him. I never heard from that guy, but I did receive an email from Richard in Irving: "Padlock looking for the right combination."

FINDING YOUR RIGHT COMBINATION

What Barbie Learned About Relationships with God and People

Everything I was learning about life, love, and relationships began with a relationship with Christ. I had accepted Christ and had surrendered everything except my dating life. I had three kids and two ex-husbands, and I just thought it was too late for me. I found it hard to believe, after all that I had been through, that God could still have a good plan for marriage for me.

Divorce is an ending, but it is also a beginning. When I got divorced, I found myself in such a strange place. I was in my late thirties, starting over again. The journey of divorce is different for everyone, but at some point we all reach a similar place—alone and wondering what is next.

The day we decide to pick ourselves up and begin a new journey can be exciting. I was so ready to see what God had for me. What I discovered is that God cared less about what I do than who I became. God wanted me to stay focused on him so he could show me who I am and all that he created me to be. All I wanted was to find a man to "complete me." The problem is, the idea of someone completing you is a lie from Hollywood.

As I ventured into the dating world, I soon learned that we cannot put God expectations on a person—that person will fail you every time. God wants us to follow him and his perfect will. God can dream a bigger dream for you than you can dream for yourself. Will you trust him?

This journey wasn't just one to get the guy; it was about learning who I am in Christ, and it all began with my relationship with Jesus. You cannot do this without him.

What God's Word Says About Relationships with God and People

The LORD your God will change your heart and the hearts of all your descendants, so that you will love him with all your heart and soul and so you may live! (Deuteronomy 30:6 NLT)

Trust in the LORD with all your heart and lean not on your own understanding; in all your ways submit to him, and he will make your paths straight. (Proverbs 3:5–6)

Those who hope in the LORD will renew their strength. They will soar on wings like eagles; they will run and not grow weary, they will walk and not be faint. (Isaiah 40:31)

The thief comes only to steal and kill and destroy. I came that they may have life and have it abundantly. (John 10:10 ESV)

If you declare with your mouth, "Jesus is Lord," and believe in your heart that God raised him from the dead, you will be saved. (Romans 10:9)

As God shows you more Scriptures that relate to your relationships with him and others, write them on this page too.

৩◎৩

Proverbs 13:20; John 15:12–15; Acts 5:29; Romans 5:8; Colossians 3:23

Begin Your Own Process

- Have you accepted Jesus as your Lord and Savior?
- Have you surrendered everything to him, or are you keeping some things for yourself?
- If you answered no to either of those questions, what are you waiting for?

You can pray a simple prayer right now:

> *Dear God, I admit that I am a sinner and that I have messed up from time to time. I believe that Jesus died on the cross for my sins and that God raised him from the dead. I choose to follow you, Jesus, and I confess that you are my Savior. Thank you, Jesus, for saving me. I love you. Amen.*

If you prayed that prayer, you just made the best decision of your life! God wants to take you places you never imagined. But maybe, like I was, you are holding on to some areas of your life that you need to give him. Talk to God. Ask him to reveal those areas and strengthen you to release them to him. Note those areas in the blank space on this page.

CHAPTER 4

Where It All Began: Richard (Part 2)

Surrender and Freedom

*Here I am in the midst of this huge storm, and
I am just holding on for dear life.*
—Richard

I FINALLY GOT TO WHERE MY BAD DECISIONS began to snowball on me. It wasn't long before I lost my apartment. By grace, a coworker offered me the extra room in his place. Though living there would put me on the opposite side of Dallas from where my daughter lived, I had no other options, so I decided I would make it work somehow and moved in.

But no sooner would I solve one problem than I'd be faced with another. My life went from bad to worse when my car got repossessed. It was one thing to get to and from work; it was another to pick up my daughter, get her to school, and return her home on the weekends I had custody of her. There was no way I could get by without my car. So I jumped through hoops to get it back, and I breathed a sigh of relief to have dodged another bullet.

Once again I found myself all messed up and feeling an undeniable pull from God. Something *had* to change. In my heart, I knew I was just one mistake away from losing everything that meant the world to me. I'd certainly felt God tap on my shoulder often enough by this time that I could no longer ignore him. I was at the end of my rope and decided I had absolutely nothing to lose in reaching out for help. I confided my decision to my girlfriend at the time and started my search for the right place to enter drug treatment.

I scoured the internet for a faith-based program to enter. I wasn't sure of much, but I was sure I wanted God to be a part of my recovery and my life going forward. I was disappointed that there weren't many options close to home, so I eventually settled on a place in upstate New York that seemed a good match for me. But it was so very far away! When I shared the news with my girlfriend, she was understandably unhappy. She wanted to be able to visit and be supportive of my efforts, so she started looking for a place that might meet both our needs.

It was about this time that I can look back and see God begin to show himself. My girlfriend located a new faith-based treatment center called Eternal Awakenings that was located a few hours south of where I was living. We were both excited and hopeful that this place could be what I needed. I looked over their website and decided to check into it with a phone call. Within a just few minutes of chatting with Jim, one of the founders, my decision was made. I knew without question that Eternal Awakenings was the place God was calling me to—the place where he would meet me and help me find a new me. I thought maybe that was where I would finally find his open arms and feel his love.

In spite of my readiness to seek out treatment and to heal, I wasn't prepared to share my decision with everyone I knew. Most of them hadn't even known I had a problem, so it seemed reasonable to hold any confessions or announcements for the backside, when I returned home. I told my mom, my sisters, and my brother, but as far as everyone else was concerned, I would be heading out for a month of training for my job. I just couldn't face the confrontation and condemnation that I antici-pated from others. I needed this time to focus on mending rather than defending myself.

I boarded my flight in Dallas and headed to Austin alone. I had no idea what to expect, but I remember feeling hopeful for the first time in a long time. I was greeted on the other end by a client from the house and a friendly woman named Karla, a cofounder at Eternal Awakenings and wife to Jim. They loaded my belongings into her car, and we began the last leg of the trip that I hoped and prayed would bring change. We headed out of town, first making a stop at a nearby convenience store for something to drink, and as we pulled into the parking lot, I immediately noticed a good-looking girl waiting in a truck nearby. Without hesitation, I looked over at Karla.

"You see that girl right there in that truck?" I asked, "That's my second drug of choice right there."

The ride lasted around an hour, and we passed the time in easy conversation that lifted my apprehension about what might lie ahead for me. Karla navigated her way through the wide-open Texas landscape and finally onto an old country dirt road where Eternal Awakenings was located—an old farmhouse surrounded by miles of maize fields. From the beginning, I felt the comfort of a welcoming home with a loving heart. I don't know if I heard it or felt it, but God was most surely there, arms open wide and whispering, "You're almost home."

Coming Out of the Storm

Jim and Karla Welch are the heart and soul of Eternal Awakenings. Recovered and sober for more than twenty years from their own addictions, they believe that connecting with the power of Jesus Christ is what lifts addicts from their dependence and restores them to their hope and healing. It was that philosophy that drew me there and encouraged me as I began a month-long journey of finding myself in God. I remember telling Karla when I arrived that I didn't feel I was there so much for the drug treatment as I was to get back what I'd really lost—my relationship with Jesus Christ. It was as if my being there had been ordained by God himself, and as the days passed, he kept showing up in so many ways, confirming time and again that I'd made the right choice in coming there. I walked in one man and left a completely different man, a man absolutely surrendered to Christ. Those days proved to be a pivotal point in my life.

Explaining why is sometimes hard. I don't share my stories with many people because they're hard to believe—like the sudden healing through the laying on of hands. There was one guy in treatment with me whom I didn't get along with well. I always got bad vibes from him and tried to keep my distance, but he was always asking me to go with him to this place where he practiced with a worship band. Each time he asked, I politely turned him down until I got myself backed into a corner and finally agreed to go with him to a place called the House of Prayer.

I was resistant and unhappy to be wasting my time with this guy, so I was already on edge when we arrived. At first, there was only me and two other guys hanging out waiting on the others, so I created some distance and ended up wandering around, trying to look busy studying all the artifacts on the walls and tables. Along one of the walls was a love seat, and above it was a picture of someone holding on to a cross in the middle of the ocean amid big waves. He was blowing like a flag in the wind, stretched out sideways with huge storm waves crashing around him as he clung to the cross. All I could do was fix my gaze in pure amazement. *That's me! Here I am in the midst of this huge storm, and I am just holding on for dear life.* Nothing could have said what I was feeling any better than that picture.

I could feel the frustration building up in me as I continued to stare at the picture. The anger that had been simmering in me for so long lay just below the surface, and it was making me uneasy. Then I noticed a bottle of anointing oil sitting on the shelf just beneath the picture, and suddenly a wave of emotion welled up within me, like an internal storm threatening to burst out. I didn't say a word out loud, but the voice was strong inside my head. *All right, God, you want to know what I want? I'm staring at this picture, and that's me. I'm in the middle of the storm of my life. So you want to be real? You want to know what I want? Well, I'll tell you what I want. I want to be anointed with that oil right there on that shelf.*

That whole time I was in my own little world as more people began to arrive and the band started warming up to begin rehearsing for worship. I continued to wander around and look at the other art and artifacts on display before I finally parked myself on the love seat beneath the picture to wait out the rehearsal.

As I sat there, I noticed a woman come in the side door. Something about her held my attention as she moved around the room, stopping to kneel and pray from time to time in different parts of the room. I continued to watch her walk around for a while before laying my head back against the wall and closing my eyes, letting go and feeling the music wash over me. Suddenly I was startled from my thoughts by the same lady tapping me on my shoulder.

Without any introduction, she asked, "Would you come with me?" Gesturing with her fingers, she told me, "God has asked me to anoint you with this oil right here on this shelf."

I was in shock as she picked up the bottle on the shelf above my head and led me to a quiet corner of the room. There, she prayed over me in tongues and anointed my head, my eyes, my ears, my feet, and my hands with the same oil that I had just challenged God to use on me. I was blown away!

Once I returned to the treatment center, I shared my experience with Karla. The whole evening had been the most incredible, personal, spiritual experience I'd ever had.

"What do you think about what happened?" she asked.

"I feel blessed," I said.

"I believe you are blessed," she said with a smile.

I went to bed that night feeling that God was clearly telling me my time here was done, my time at the center was drawing to a close, and my time with him had begun.

The remaining days of my treatment passed quickly, and I spent each one digging deeper into my healing and opening my arms wider to God. I continued to have big aha moments and encounters that I can only credit to God working in me. A day didn't pass without a reminder to me that I was better than I thought I was, that God wanted me to have his best if only I would embrace it. He showed me myself and my life like I was looking at a movie. I became aware of the negative attitudes and behaviors that were impacting me and others. I knew I was being changed forever, that a miracle was happening in me. I felt like I was looking at life through a new pair of eyes. But as my time in treatment came to a close, I wondered how I was going to live as the new me out there in a world that probably hadn't changed very much.

While commitment in my relationships had never been one of my strengths, I had no problem in owning the fact that if I was going to achieve spiritual maturity, I had no choice but to completely surrender myself to Christ. So before I walked out of treatment, I made the decision to give myself up to him 110 percent. I knew that I could no longer give him bits and pieces. This had to be one of those all-or-nothing deals if I was going to make the change stick outside the walls of this safe place.

That was my turning point. I gave it all up, including sex, and decided that if I was going to live by one of God's rules, I had to live by them all.

Where the Rubber Meets the Road

Change is great until you take it out for a spin in the real world. I walked out the door of Eternal Awakenings excited about a new life and a new me, but I'd forgotten to make allowances for the fact that absolutely nothing on the outside had changed since I left.

The most difficult challenge I faced was in my relationship with my girlfriend. The idea of a new me was great until I actually showed up. Even though she had supported my rehab and had visited me every weekend, she clearly wasn't able to understand how God was changing me. She definitely didn't see it coming when I walked back into the relationship with new rules.

We were talking one evening, and I thought we needed to get a few things straight. When we'd been together before treatment, we'd had a typical relationship where we often spent the night with each other. That wasn't part of the deal for me anymore, and I had to tell her I wouldn't be staying over. I tried to reassure her that we were still a couple, but I knew she was confused.

At first she was okay with the new arrangements. It was like, new you, new me, new time, new beginning. But very quickly that faded, and she wanted to know when we were getting back to where we had left off. What we had now felt like just friends to her, like we were going nowhere. She wanted a good man but not necessarily the way I was proposing it to her. It was tough for me to understand that the structure of our new relationship wasn't working for her, and I didn't know how to let it go. She had been so instrumental in getting me to and through my rehab and was a big part of my becoming the man I now was. But I just knew in my gut that I had to give up controlling the outcome.

I finally left it to God, and I prayed that he would show me if our relationship wasn't meant to be. I told him that if this wasn't part of his plan, he needed to close the door, because I didn't know how. So I did the biggest thing I could do—I proposed to her and left the rest in God's hands. I was prepared for anything.

The night I proposed, I immediately sensed a lack of excitement. She accepted the ring, but when I went back to see her the very next day, the ring was sitting on the end table.

"You didn't even wear that to work, did you?" I asked.

She quietly replied, "No."

"That's all I needed to know," I replied.

We shared a brief conversation, and I took the ring, walking out her door and out of her life. I never looked back. I remember driving off looking out the sunroof of my car and literally thanking God out loud. I knew that if it hadn't fallen apart then, it would have fallen apart later. I didn't even feel very sad. Chapter closed.

I totally get how some people fall off the wagon once they return to the real world. You aren't the same person, but you return to the same people and the same challenges you had before you changed. It would be so much easier if you could start from scratch, you know, with new people who weren't framing you with old expectations. Everyone you know, even your family, doesn't really know what to do with the new you. They are suspicious of you and look at you with doubt. I guess they want to believe, but it's like it's too good to be true. I have a vivid recollection of my ex-wife saying to me, "Who are you? I don't even know who you are anymore."

Someone once told me that going back home after treatment is like replacing a broken tube in a wind chime. Even though you've been out of tune, the people in your life are accustomed to the unique sound you have together. When you're "repaired" and replaced, they are uncomfortable. The beautiful music of the chimes is returned, but you are making a different sound and it affects them. Your changes make them think about their own stuff. Even those closest to you, the ones you thought would take the most joy in your changes, have a hard time knowing what to do with the new you.

Besides, a new you doesn't necessarily make a perfect you. I faced lots of unexpected challenges, and old temptations often popped back up, luring me to cozy up in familiar surroundings. I did well with most of it; I held close to God and what I knew he wanted for me. The commitment in my sexual life was the easiest one to keep. For a brief while, I fell back into the drugs; mostly, I was curious if I could handle them, and I still wanted the rush and the way the meth blurred the rough edges when things weren't going like I'd hoped they would. So for about a month, I picked up where I left off. But wouldn't you know it—God stepped in again with that pesky tapping on my shoulder. In his still, small voice, he reminded me that I served a bigger God, and he had a plan for me. I tossed my stuff and never touched it again.

Revelation keeps coming when you're healing from addiction, and one of the biggest hurdles I faced on the outside was forgiveness, not so much of others but for myself. I had to take responsibility for the trail of pain that had resulted from my past choices—women I'd used, people I'd introduced to drugs, broken commitments, lies. The remorse and guilt I felt over how my actions might have completely changed the direction of another person's life was a painful burden. I found myself trying to make up for the wrongs. Sometimes the load was heavy.

I can only say I'm grateful that God continued to show up in my life and lead me when I needed it most. My ability to make amends for so many years of hurt seemed insurmountable until the Word of God once again whispered in my ear during a sermon at my church. In spite of having asked for forgiveness and forgiving others, I had yet to forgive myself. The sermon was called *Forgiveness: The Real F-Word*. In it, our pastor told a story of a time he'd seen a dog tied to a bench. When something startled the dog, it had suddenly taken off running, dragging the bench behind him. The bench had bounced along behind the dog, hitting a car and a few other things before the owner in the store realized what was happening and was able to untie his dog from the bench. He reminded us that unforgiveness was like that bench. You drag it around behind you, and it causes all kinds of collateral damage in your life.

I sat there thinking, asking myself and God who it was that I hadn't yet forgiven that was still tied to my bench. Like a light bulb going off, I realized it was me. I was tied to my own bench! Here I had asked for forgiveness from everyone in my life, but I had yet to forgive myself. In that moment, God reminded me that it was time to lay all my concerns at the foot of the cross, to give that heavy burden to him. I felt like a fifty-pound weight had been lifted from my chest, and in my mind, I imagined myself wiping my hands clean. Sitting there, I truly accepted the gift of grace that could propel me forward to the next place in my life.

Much as I wished for the path ahead to be smooth sailing from there, it wasn't. I had so much work to do. But I began to clearly see the pieces of a new life begin to fall into place. Little by little, I was freed from the chains that had held me back from pursuing God's purpose for my life. Clinging to my commitment for change and my faith that he was directing my feet, I continued to move forward one step at a time.

After the breakup with my girlfriend, I didn't jump back into the dating world for a long time. I'd begun to learn that it's a long road from making the decision to date God's way to actually trusting yourself to do it. There was some security in holding back; it was easier to avoid mistakes. I didn't want to backslide in a moment of weakness. Sex had been a big part of how I defined myself as a man, and I knew I needed to rein myself in and focus on other things for a while.

My plan worked for me, but it was driving others in my life to distraction. When you aren't dating, the whole world thinks there's something wrong. I was constantly getting offers to be set up with a nice girl. The people have good intentions, but their efforts and encouragement don't always help. It takes a lot longer for your friends and family to realize you are no longer the "broken chime" and to embrace your change.

When I finally decided to put myself out there and get my feet wet again, I was careful to stay in casual one- or two-date situations. If it went beyond that, I felt the need to announce my decision to remain sexually pure so the women I dated were clear that I had a plan for myself. The crazy part was that, in our culture, we always assume it is the guys who are expecting sex, but I encountered expectations from the women after only a few dates. I don't think they came from the same place a man does. For them, I think it had much more to do with receiving validation that they are attractive and desirable. Rather than interpreting my choice of dating God's way as one of valuing myself and her, it somehow contorted into an attack on her self-esteem. It was a stumbling block I never expected to encounter.

I worked hard and with intention to find a new dating rhythm through the better part of the next five years. I hoped there would be somebody out there who would appreciate and honor the choices I'd made, but what I found were a lot of women who bailed after I didn't come through when they thought I should. To my disappointment, I found this to be the case even among Christian women who I thought might share my belief.

After a while, my well-meaning mom and sisters hounded me to get on with it so I could find someone I could marry and start a family with. By now I was in my forties, and they thought it was time to move on with my life. I knew they didn't understand, but I held my ground, trusting that this journey was taking me to the right woman at the right time.

The good news was that the experiences of those years taught me a whole new way of relating to the opposite sex. I learned to appreciate their finer qualities. I learned to have a conversation and get to know them beyond the surface of appearances and my instinctive drives. For the first time in my life, I saw God working in me to see the women in my life through new eyes of respect and honor. Little did I know he was laying the foundation for a long-term dating relationship that would ultimately end in marriage.

A little before spring break, I decided to post in Yahoo! Personals and see who turned up on my match list. Believing I needed to say something that set me apart from the pack, I wrote, "Padlock looking for the right combination."

And then, Barbie happened.

FINDING YOUR RIGHT COMBINATION

What Richard Learned About Surrender and Freedom

Richard always says, "We can commit our lives to Christ and accept him as our Lord and Savior, but not *surrendering* to him keeps us in spiritual immaturity."

Richard was doing what he wanted, when he wanted, how he wanted. But his daily decisions that he thought were freedom were actually keeping him in bondage. Our culture would have us believe that what's good for you is good for you, and what's good for me is good for me. God gives us free will, and we have the ability to choose how we live our life, but not all things are beneficial. Just because you *can* doesn't mean you *should*. The satisfaction of the moment has consequences.

I love watching Richard now, with his passion for mentoring men and for prison ministry. He gets to speak into the lives of men who are in literal bondage and share with them the freedom that is found through Jesus Christ.

Sadly, many of us are in a prison of our own making. Our comfort zone is not always comfortable; it is just what we know. Fear is not from God. Have the courage to make a new decision and surrender your life to the one who calms the seas and brings you peace. If you are dealing with addiction, as Richard was, I encourage you to take the brave step and seek faith-based treatment.

What God's Word Says About Surrender and Freedom

The fear of the LORD is the beginning of knowledge, but fools despise wisdom and instruction. (Proverbs 1:7)

If the Son sets you free, you will be free indeed. (John 8:36)

"I have the right to do anything," you say—but not everything is beneficial. "I have the right to do anything"—but not everything is constructive. (1 Corinthians 10:23)

When I was a child, I spoke as a child, I understood as a child, I thought as a child; but when I became a man, I put away childish things. (1 Corinthians 13:11 NKJV)

If anyone is a hearer of the word and not a doer, he is like a man observing his natural face in a mirror; for he observes himself, goes away, and immediately forgets what kind of man he was. (James 1:23–24 NKJV)

As God shows you more Scriptures that relate to your relationships with him and others, write them on this page too.

෮◉෮

Luke 9:23–24; Romans 12:2; James 4:7, 10; 1 Peter 5:6–10

Begin Your Own Process

- Are there things in your life, good or bad, that are keeping you stuck?
- What would you lose by letting go of what is holding you back?
- What decision can you make today to move forward?

There can often be habits in our lives that are not good for us, but we hold on to them out of our fear of the unknown. Other times, we might hold on to habits that we see as good, and we allow the comfort of familiarity and the fear that we will be unable to find something better hold us back from reaching for the goodness of our God, who stands waiting to give us so much more. I want to encourage you to look back on your answers to the questions and begin to dream about what your life of freedom might look like. Spend some time with God in prayer and journal about your dreams and his directions. God can dream a bigger dream for you than you can dream for yourself.

PART 2

THE DECISION BEFORE THE DECISION: COMPARING NOTES WITH BARBIE AND RICHARD

GOING FORWARD, RICHARD AND I tell the story of our dating relationship together, sharing and comparing notes on topics vital to growing our relationship until we both were ready to say, "I do!" Our hope is that you will find encouragement and godly takeaways for discovering your own right combination.

CHAPTER 5

Who Am I?

Identity in Christ and Boundaries in Dating

Do you know you're beautiful?
—Barbie's Counselor

Barbie

GOING THROUGH A DIVORCE left me wondering, *Who am I now? How do I like to wear my hair? What's my favorite style of dress? What kinds of things do I enjoy doing in my free time? What do I believe? What's important to me?*

My identity was so wrapped up in my old life as a wife and mother that I didn't even think about who I was or what I enjoyed anymore. I had never really been on my own before, having moved from my parent's home into my first marriage, and then later into my second marriage quickly following the first divorce. The last clear picture I had of myself alone was of an eighteen-year-old girl with big dreams of heading to London to train at Vidal Sassoon and of building a career as a platform artist.

I tossed those dreams aside when the prospect of marrying the first time came up. Having a husband and a family was my other dream, and as life sometimes happens, the dream job meant long hours, travel, and a lifestyle that would never mesh with life as a suburban wife and certainly not as a stay-at-home mom. I never went to London, but I landed a job as a stylist in a local Aveda salon. God is so good though. What looked like a sacrifice on the surface turned out to be a long career that I loved in the beauty industry.

Being on my own after my second divorce meant going back to work to support myself and my kids, and I returned to the comfort of the beauty industry, this time managing a spa in a high-end gym in Dallas. I was good at my job, and I enjoyed being surrounded by creatives. One of the upsides of being back in familiar territory was that it reminded me of the fun, stylish girl I'd been in my twenties, and I happily opened up to finding myself all over again. I began experimenting with style and changed the way I dressed to a little less conservatively. I also opted for a dramatic change of hairstyle from my medium-length, curly hair to a straight, short bob cut. I loved it! It felt so good to reinvent myself—to become a new me, though in hindsight maybe I was just becoming *more* me. I was emerging from my cocoon, no longer wrapped up in the opinions and preferences of someone else.

Crossroads

The walk I began with Christ during my second marriage was still new, and I continued to spend time in prayer as I navigated my way into my new life. I trusted that God would bring the boys and me through our troubles and into better days, and I surrendered every area of my life to him. At least I thought I did.

When it came to relationships with men, however, I believed I had it all under control. Don't get me wrong—I prayed God would bring the right man to our family. But I never once consulted him about whether I should go out with someone or how I should conduct myself when I did.

I was never what I'd call promiscuous, but I had a couple of male friendships that ended up being more like friends with benefits. It was easy to justify that I was not, at least, sleeping around. Plus, it wasn't like I was a virgin with her virtue to protect. I was a twice-divorced woman and a mother, for goodness' sake.

But as time passed, I began to feel God quietly challenging me. I would stand looking into the mirror in the bathroom of a nightclub, and the questions would float through my head. *Why am I here? Whose life is this? Is this what I'm supposed to be doing?* I couldn't help but feel that God was asking me if my walk with him was aligned with my choices, and even though I heard his words, I didn't see another way to meet someone new. I was lonely.

Of course, sex was always a hot topic and the focus of many conversations between me and my single girlfriends. Whether we were divorced or never married, when we shared observations about dating, it would inevitably come up that we wanted a guy who was not just looking to get us into bed. We wanted someone who wanted to get to actually know us. I didn't know, after all I had been through, if that kind of man even existed, but I was so hopeful when I met Richard. He seemed genuinely different and totally committed to his vow of waiting for sex until marriage. While I found him oddly confusing at times, I was also inexplicably drawn to him. He was different, and the difference intrigued me. After only a couple of dates, I thought he could, just maybe, be the kind of guy I had dreamed of finding, but I don't think I was prepared for the challenges he would ultimately pose and the work that God would do in me through him.

I had a good feeling about Richard and an amazing connection with him from the very beginning. Richard had a strength about him that made me feel safe, and at the same time, he was the most fun, outgoing man I'd ever dated. He brought out a side of me I'd forgotten, and I had not laughed so hard and so often in a really long time. He had a spirit of joy that was so contagious that I wanted to be with him all the time. So I set my sights on Richard and was on a mission to find out if he could be "the one."

In the weeks that followed, Richard and I talked almost every day, and we went out most weekends that we didn't have our kids, though not nearly as much as I would have liked. We had long conversations and covered almost every imaginable topic. I was all starry-eyed every time I heard from or saw him. And while I was pretty sure Richard was enjoying our time together as much as I was, I didn't quite know for sure. I had taken my online dating profile down after the end of my seven-day trial, but Richard's was still live, and I couldn't help wondering how many women he was dating other than me. It was crazy to expect him to be exclusive, but a girl could hope, right?

The no-sex thing, while I admired and respected it, made me a little uneasy. Richard's boundaries were crystal clear and set in stone. I'd find myself thinking what a great guy he was on one hand while questioning whether he found me attractive on the other. Even though I thought his actions were nice and what I thought I wanted, it felt strangely unsettling that Richard wasn't coming on to me. It was a language I had no idea how to interpret. My only frame of reference prior to going out with him was to measure my desirability according to a guy's sexual attraction to me. If I couldn't tempt Richard into having sex, did that mean I wasn't pretty or interesting? I didn't want to end up in the friend zone; I feared finding myself there. Surely if Richard found me attractive, I would know.

It didn't help my cause when many of my girlfriends, even my Christian girlfriends, confirmed my worst fears. When they found out Richard and I were not having sex, they were quick to tell me, "He's just not that into you. You're wasting your time." I was crushed by their pronouncements, but I was also confused. Weren't these the same girls who thought the perfect guy was the one who was interested in more than just sex? I had no clue what to do with all the mixed messages being sent my way.

Richard

Isn't This What Women Want?

When a guy doesn't want to have sex after only a few dates, it's crazy how women, including Barbie, are so thrown off.

Okay, maybe I should say that differently. It wasn't that I didn't want to have sex; sure I did. But I also had this clear picture of something else I wanted even more—something much bigger and more important—and of how I wanted to get there if I got into another long-term relationship.

I wanted someone to journey beside me for all the celebrations and sadness life brings us. I wanted someone who would walk with me, encourage me, and support me. I knew that I had to take my time finding the woman I would finally allow to stand in that place, and I believed the woman who was right for me would understand and respect my boundaries, including no sex outside of marriage.

Don't women say they want a man who respects them for who they are and doesn't just see them as sex objects? I wasn't looking for a good time anymore. Been there and done that, you know. I'd lived life my way for a really long time, and as far as I could see, I didn't have much to show for it. Now I had a purpose, and I wasn't wasting time dating anyone I didn't think I could marry someday. My pastor talks about us needing to make the decision before the decision. We have to know who we are, what we want, what our boundaries are, and stick to those boundaries. Once things with a woman are getting hot and heavy, it's a little late to be thinking about abstinence.

By the time Barbie's cute face popped onto my computer screen, I felt I finally had my head and my heart in the right place—that I could go out and open myself up to more in a relationship than I'd allowed since I left treatment. I wanted to date with the purpose of finding that special someone God had out there for me. I wanted someone to do life with, someone to share special moments with, and I wasn't settling for less.

Barbie

Who Wants to Be "Back Out There" After Divorce?

I really liked Richard, and I could already see myself building a life with him, but I didn't have the key to this relationship yet. We all think there's some magic formula to conjure up a happily-ever-after ending, don't we? I realized that sex had always been the key I had used to draw myself in close, and I didn't have that option with Richard. In spite of the surge of confidence I'd felt as I morphed into a hip, cute woman, this no-sex thing produced an intense insecurity in me. Was I pretty enough? Was I sexy enough? Was I . . . enough? I couldn't figure out another way to Richard's heart and his undying devotion, and it was driving me crazy.

In my efforts to figure out Richard, and because I was never 100 percent sure of his level of interest in or commitment to me, I frequently checked the status of his dating profile. Given my fears, you can imagine how excited I was when, after just a short time of seeing each other, Richard's online dating profile had been removed. I did not expect him to take it down. I read all kinds of meaning into it, because I was exclusively dating him and happy to keep it that way. *Did this mean he had decided to be exclusive with me too?* It was easy for me to interpret some happily-ever-after into his deactivated profile, even though we'd never once had a conversation about being exclusive.

Feeling a confidence boost from the imagined commitment that taking his profile down prompted, I texted him one afternoon with an invitation to join me on a local patio for happy hour. Within a couple of hours, we were together. Again we had a great conversation and enjoyed a beautiful evening outdoors. This was one of my favorite places to get together, and I was excited that he enjoyed it too. *Check. Another thing we have in common.* Overall, I couldn't help feeling pretty good about where this relationship might be going.

Unfortunately, I was in for a surprise when I arrived home that evening. I logged into my computer to kill some time before going to bed, and for some reason went straight to the dating site. I couldn't believe what I was seeing. Even though we'd been having such a great time on our dates, including that very night, he had put his profile back online— with updated photos. *What does that mean?* He had told me before that he didn't "multidate." Had I done something wrong? Said something wrong? This was not a good scenario for an overthinker like me. *Oh my goodness! Who wants to be "back out there" in their forties?*

Every possible insecurity rose up in me that night as I imagined him deciding that I wasn't what he was looking for in a woman. Like little mice on that wheel that never stops spinning, my mind circled through every possible reason why he would come back from a date with me and put himself back on the market. I knew I didn't have the right to ask, but I just couldn't let it go, so I came right out and laid it out on the table the next time I saw him. "Somehow I knew you would see that," he said, a little sheepishly. That wasn't the answer I was hoping for. Was he really hoping I wouldn't see it? I didn't want to seem needy, so I had to gather up my courage for a right response. I knew that just because I wasn't see-ing anyone else, I couldn't ask him to do the same just a couple of months in. I just hoped he wouldn't want to. A girl can hope!

Instead, I put on my couldn't-care-less attitude and told him I needed to know if that was how it was going to be—just be straight about your intentions. We agreed we were still open to date other people, but I was so discouraged. I had no intention of dating anyone else as long as he was interested in me. Now I'd just have to wait for him to come around or fig-ure out a way to convince him that I was the one for him. I don't think he believed I was okay with dating around anymore than I believed it myself.

"Who Are You Doing This For?"

Richard continued to call, and we saw each other almost every week, but we went forward like we were just friends. We met a couple of times for lunch, and we enjoyed an occasional happy hour, but there was not any-thing happening between us that I would normally use as a barometer for measuring the success of a romantic relationship. There was usually no touching or hand holding, but on occasion, Richard would give me a surprise kiss at the end of a date. I did discover after some time that if we went to a movie, he might put his hand on my leg or hold my hand, so I enjoyed going to the movies. I had feelings I had not had since high school. The little things gave me butterflies in my stomach. The feelings that normally fade after you become physical did not go away. I was so excited, and my heart would race each time I saw him.

✿

Who are you doing this for, Barbie? Me or Richard? What? I was standing in my bedroom in the middle of the day, and suddenly I heard God speaking to me. It wasn't audible, but I heard the words plain as day. I knew without explanation that he was asking me why I was agreeing to forgo the sexual part of my relationship with Richard.

If this doesn't work out, what are you going to do next time? What if the next guy doesn't want to wait? I knew the answer immediately. I *was* doing this for Richard—for his approval, to prove my devotion, to encourage him to choose me. And I knew what would happen if there was a next time with another guy. I'd be all in to do whatever it took to make him happy. I realized how much I was willing to give up of myself to be wanted by a man, and for the first time, I wondered how much of myself I'd been willing to compromise to feel loved, beautiful, and worthy.

But what now? Am I ready to make this decision? Okay God, I'm doing this! I got on my knees right there in my bedroom in the middle of the day and surrendered everything to God that I'd been holding back. I was a Christian before that day, and I had been leaning into him with all that I had, with the exception of my dating life. In spite of my two divorces, I had held on to the belief that somehow my path to a new love was still best. But in that moment I made a new choice. I was now committed to the idea of saving sex for marriage for my own reasons, and I knew if Richard suddenly changed his mind and wanted to have sex, I would say no. It's not worth it.

Now the commitment was between me and God. I felt such a sense of relief and peace and was so grateful for God's presence in that moment. I knew this was something I could never do in my own strength.

Good morning! So, God and I had a great conversation that I
will have to tell you about! It was really good!! XXOO
—Barbie's Email to Richard

What? . . . God said you need to have sex . . . and now you
have to convince me?? . . . HaHaHa!
—Richard's Email to Barbie

Note to self: *Holy cow! He is not making this any easier. One*
thing I know for sure—if God ever lets me marry him, it will
be worth the wait!

Finally! Yesterday Richard and I went on a picnic, it was
perfect! We found a cute park in Addison and had great
weather, and comfortable conversation. He had said we were
just friends getting to know each other, but the kiss he gave
me when he left said otherwise. That kiss just left me wanting
more. He called later to tell me what a good time he had, and
he took his dating profile down again. I just want to leave it in
God's hands. His plans are always better than mine.
—Barbie's Journal

FINDING YOUR RIGHT COMBINATION

What Richard and I Learned About Identity in
Christ and Boundaries in Dating

After my divorce I found myself unsure of who I was, so I went searching for my identity. The process wasn't easy, but what I eventually discovered was that my true sense of love and freedom came when I found my identity and value vertically—from God.

I had a pattern in my life of trying to be who I believed others wanted me to be, whether or not it was authentic. It took me a long time, and a few mistakes along the way, to understand that what truly satisfies my soul is what God says about me. He says I am his beloved daughter, that I am wonderfully made, that I am more than a conqueror, and that he has a good plan for my life.

Who you believe you are affects every boundary in your life, including your dating life—especially sex outside of marriage. When Richard found his identity in Christ, he became a new creation, and he totally devoted himself to obedience and taking his guidance from God's Word.

Richard moved forward with confidence that the boundaries God set in place would ultimately be for his good, and he stood firm no matter what. Richard chose to be very intentional in dating. He made sure we dated in public to avoid temptation. We did not spend time with one another's kids in the beginning. And he was always honest about where he stood in our relationship.

I struggled with the no-sex boundary in a different way than Richard because I had always found my approval and my identity through other people. I can't think of any place a person can get more instant validation from another human being than during sex. But the feelings of "intimacy" and "love" were only temporary, and I was always left with guilt and shame. I had to stop begging other people to tell me who I am and trust who God says I am so I could move forward into the life he has planned for me. When we permit another person to give us our identity and value, we also give that person permission to take them away.

The same goes for boundaries. Had I continued to let Richard set the boundaries when it came to sex, he could have decided to move the boundaries. Once I committed to God, my boundaries were firm regardless of Richard's choices.

God's ways work. He is a loving father who has his very best for you; we are the ones who settle. He made you perfectly, and don't let anyone tell you any different. You are enough!

What God's Word Says About Identity in Christ and Boundaries in Dating

I praise you because I am fearfully and wonderfully made; your works are wonderful, I know that full well. (Psalm 139:14)

You are altogether beautiful, my darling, beautiful in every way. (Song of Solomon 4:7 NLT)

In all these things we are more than conquerors through Him who loved us. (Romans 8:37 NKJV)

He chose us in [Christ] before the creation of the world to be holy and blameless in his sight. (Ephesians 1:4)

Let perseverance finish its work, so that you may be mature and complete, not lacking anything. (James 1:4)

As God shows you more Scriptures that relate to your identity in Christ and boundaries in dating, write them on this page too.

෨෧෨

Jeremiah 29:11; Amos 3:3; 2 Corinthians 6:14–18; 1 Timothy 5:1–2; Hebrews 13:4

Begin Your Own Process

- Do you feel worthy of having the kind of relationship you've always dreamed of? Why or why not?
- How does the way you see yourself compare to the way God sees you?
- What are your thoughts on abstinence as a part of dating God's way?

Whether or not you're currently dating, take some time to write down the boundaries you need to establish in order to date God's way. God made you perfectly and on purpose. It is never too late to have and be all that he has for you. You have to make the decision before the decision. You can't wait until you are on the couch making out to decide not to have sex. Pray for God to give you the courage to communicate those boundaries well, and stick to them when the time is appropriate.

CHAPTER 6

Life Renovation

Restoration and Waiting

It's demo day!
—Chip Gaines

Barbie

WHEN I FOUND MYSELF trying to put my life back together with my boys, my vision for our future was simply to reclaim what I felt I'd lost. To get us back to the place we'd been before. It never occurred to me that God would use my divorce to do some major life renovations.

My post-divorce life was like one of those home renovation shows on TV, where they take an old house and turn it into somebody's dream home. They start with something broken down and demo it back to the framework. But when they rebuild it, they don't just make it what it once was; they make it even more amazing. This is what it felt like God was doing in my life: getting rid of all the broken-down "stuff" and refining and preparing me to be and do abundantly more than I could ever dream.

Restoration

The first place I found God beginning to put our life back together was when I decided to leave my business behind and return to the beauty industry. I knew that building on my strengths would get me a lot further in less time than trying to do something new. And being back in familiar territory helped me get back a confidence I had lost. I started out managing a spa, but my knowledge could take me in several different directions. I felt I would eventually be able to provide for myself and the boys and begin rebuilding our life.

One of the most important struggles I faced was in providing a home of our own. Making the move from self-employed to having a "real" job opened the door to all of that happening, and I soon found myself searching for the perfect house.

I'm not sure how I found this precious neighborhood, but as soon as we pulled in past the beautiful magnolia trees, I knew I was home. I had visited the model home in the neighborhood and described to the sales guy what I was looking for, so he took me to several homes that were nice, but they weren't quite right. Finally, he said, "Okay, I have one more I think might be the one," and we piled back in the car.

When we pulled up in front of the last house, I said nothing, but he could tell from my face that he'd finally gotten my attention. "Did the clouds part?" he asked. *Yes, I think they did.*

In the coming months, we settled into our new home and a new routine, and I spent more time focusing on my kids, my friends, and my family. We were surrounded by amazing neighbors who stepped in and helped me with my kids and became our extended family. My favorite place became my front porch swing, where I loved spending time with God and good friends and, more than anything, hearing the words, "Mom, watch!" as my boys did their latest tricks on a skateboard or a bike. I finally felt like God was restoring our family and our life on so many levels.

> *God picked me up out of my old life and put me in Savannah,*
> *Texas. He gave me new friends, gave my boys a new school,*
> *and I am so blessed.*
> —Barbie's Journal

"Why Are You Church Hopping?"

My last real holdout was finding a church home. By the time I met Richard, my sons and I had visited several churches in search of a new spiritual home. Since we moved so far from where we previously lived, I had focused my attention on several smaller congregations in the area but hadn't felt the tug to commit to any of them. Truthfully, avoiding the decision to choose a church was really just me procrastinating so I wouldn't have to deal with everything that might come with it. Once I made a decision, I would actually have to do something, right? I guess, more than anything, I worried about being divorced twice. I mean, what would people think?

A few months before meeting Richard, my boys and I had begun visiting the Fellowship Church Grapevine location, which just happened to be the church Richard attended. Michael and Dalton immediately loved it! The kids' programs engaged them to learn about the Lord through fun activities and music. One walk down the children's hall area and even us grown-ups wanted a peek into the classrooms to see what all the noise was about.

I enjoyed it as well, but it was a really big church, and I had a hard time seeing how I might fit in there. I was afraid, with my limited church experience as well as my past, that I would not have many opportunities to serve, and I was hoping to find a church where I could give back. On the weekends when I didn't have my boys, I continued to visit churches closer to my house, just in case I found something I liked better.

I could see that Richard clearly loved his church, and we often talked about it over dinner. One night he challenged me to attend the newcomer's class to learn more about the church and to see if it was a good fit for me and the boys.

"Why are you church hopping?" he asked.

What? I was a little taken aback, I mean, I wouldn't call what we were doing church *hopping.* I would say it was more like church *shopping.* There was a difference, right? Either way, his words made me stop and think about how I was doing this, so I took his advice and signed up for the next newcomer's class.

In the class I learned about the church's history and all the amazing things that Fellowship Church had done and was doing. The whole time, I felt a sense of excitement that I was in the right place, and I couldn't wait for the woman who was speaking to finish because I had an over-whelming sense that I *needed* to talk to her. As soon as I could, I made my way forward to introduce myself. I shared with her a little bit about myself and how I was looking for a church home—a place where I could get involved in women's ministry.

Without hesitation, she said, "I don't know if this would interest you, but we're doing a dinner at the women's shelter in Fort Worth and could use some volunteers. Are you interested in something like that?"

Absolutely! This is the same place I went to for counseling during my divorce. So many women had come alongside me through my divorce, and I had been looking for some way to give back to them for all they had done to help me. This seemed like the perfect opportunity. It was sud-denly so clear that this church and this ministry were home. I decided in that moment to join the church, and I could hardly wait to tell Richard that he had been so right to encourage me to attend the class. I felt like God was putting the pieces of my life back together. I had a great job and a beautiful home. Now I had a church too!

Richard

You're Trying Too Hard

Listening to Barbie share about her experience at the newcomer's class over dinner at Esparza's, I could tell how excited she was about Fellow-ship Church. Although I had challenged her to check out the church, I wasn't expecting her to jump right in and be so excited. I don't know why. I loved my church, and I knew she would too. Nonetheless, I felt like she was trying too hard to get close to me, and it made me uncomfortable.

We still didn't know each other all that well—and honestly, I was probably sending some mixed messages.

I mean, I liked my church and was happy she did too, but it felt like "my" church. Church was a sacred place that I'd only really shared with my daughter up to this moment. I realized Barbie had been attending there off and on before she knew me, but her enthusiastic presence now felt like an invasion of sorts. I had an all-too-familiar feeling that I'd had with girls I'd dated in the past. You go out, and the next thing you know, you can't get rid of them. Then again, I hadn't been out in the dating scene with my new rules all that long, and my panic was probably due to how women responded to my old behavior patterns. In the past, I didn't think twice about hooking up with a woman right away, and the lines would get blurred. She would get the wrong message (now I know I *was* sending the wrong message), and all of a sudden, she would think there was more to the relationship than there was.

However, even though I wasn't dating like that anymore, the old feelings of panic would pop up all the same. At the same time, having Barbie "invade" my space felt like growth. I knew God wanted to grow me, and I would have to get a little uncomfortable.

I was also struggling with how all my worlds were starting to collide. Before Barbie, my church was *my* church; my time with my daughter was *my* time; my time with my family was *my* time. Now I'd entered this universe where all things were starting to come together. I knew in my head that this was what was supposed to happen, but I felt it was all happening too fast, and it made me way too uncomfortable. It didn't help that Daylee and my family were each asking, "What happened to our time?"

So I remained at a distance with Barbie, still protecting myself and my other worlds. However, others at the church could clearly see that Barbie and I were dating, and the more I tried to keep space between us, the more they encouraged me to take a risk. The thought of being vulnerable and opening myself up to getting hurt again was scary, but as uncomfortable as putting myself out there could be, the possibilities were also exciting. Even though I had come to know who I was in Christ and was absolutely content with who and where I was, I also felt the need to have that special someone in my life to share special moments with. I guess sometimes we get so content we forget how to take risks.

Barbie

It's Not About You

When I shared my experience at the newcomer's class with Richard, he told me I was trying too hard.

Are you serious? My boys and I had been attending Fellowship as visitors way before we ever knew who he was. All he'd done was suggest a class so I'd know if it was the right church for us. What I knew for sure was that I couldn't let Richard be the reason I joined the church, but I also couldn't let him be the reason I didn't.

The boys and I joined Fellowship and jumped into classes and volunteer opportunities whenever we could. After my conversation with Richard, I was careful to stay independent and keep some space between the areas where I volunteered and where Richard volunteered. I had no way of knowing where my relationship with him would go, but I knew I needed to plant myself in order to be strong here, with or without him. I never wanted this to be the church I used to go to with Richard; I wanted a home for my family.

I was super excited when I received a card in the mail from Richard. "I just want to congratulate you on your decision to join the body of Christ (the local church). I know he will bless you and your family in your decision. I give thanks and praise to God for allowing me to be a part of his already perfect plan."

Talk about a change of heart!

Holy moly! Richard is amazing! He may or may not be the guy
God intends for me, but already I see how he is using Richard

*to point me to him. Whatever happens, I am so glad the boys
and I joined Fellowship Church.*
—Barbie's Journal

"What Do You Think?"

I continued giving my relationship with Richard to God and trusting that God would put the two of us together when and if he wanted us together. He'd already done it more times than I could count. I had become very intentional about serving in areas at church where Richard wasn't, though I would get an occasional phone call to serve in an area I knew he served in. I was a little worried that if I said yes, Richard would think I was trying to invade his space. I called him and he said it was fine. I had my doubts but did say yes. If this was where God wanted me, who was I to argue?

After my boys and I had been attending and serving at Fellowship for a while, I got a call from one of the pastors. He wanted to talk to me about leading a singles group that met in homes to do Bible studies. I was a little surprised by the call but very excited. He shared what leading would entail, but he left out one detail. I asked if I would have a colead. *Hint, hint.* He said I would and wanted to know if I had anyone in mind. Of course I did! He said he assumed that I might but wanted to make sure I was okay with it before he contacted Richard.

I waited for Richard to tell me that he had also heard from the pastor. "What do you think?" I asked a little anxiously. "I think it will be awesome," he told me. *Okay, let's do this!* I was so excited to be able to lead with Richard. I just knew God was bringing us together.

Richard

All in God's Timing

I didn't know whether Barbie was orchestrating our time together at church or whether God was really behind it, bringing us together.

Nonetheless, there was no doubt about the feelings I was getting from her on the relationship side of things. To me it felt like she was trying too hard. Don't get me wrong—I loved having her around. I just wanted to take my time and enjoy the process. The last thing I wanted to do was rush things. I wanted to get to know one another, get to know her boys, and make sure Barbie was the woman God had for me.

I had already seen what happened when I tried to do things my way. This time around, I was committed to following God's lead. I might have been overly cautious, but I felt there was a lot at stake. She had two boys who lived with her, and I had a daughter. It was hard blending families. Top that off with the fact that according to a message from my pastor, 67 percent of second marriages and 73 percent of third marriages end in divorce. So I was set on taking my time. I had seen too many friends, including church friends, rush into relationships only to find out it wasn't really what they wanted. Taking it slow and easy was what I intended to do.

Barbie

Sanctuary

Some areas of my life seemed on fast-forward; other areas, such as my relationship with Richard, not so much. What I knew for sure was that my boys and I were so blessed. I loved living in my sweet neighborhood. I don't know what I would have done without the amazing neighbors who came alongside me. They helped me with my boys and gave me back a sense of community. God knew exactly where I needed to live. My friends, including Richard, thought I lived too far from civilization, so they didn't come over often. I didn't mind. It was my retreat, my sanctuary, and exactly where I needed to be at this time in my life.

As a single mom, I didn't always find it easy to keep up with everything, but I worked really hard at it. Expenses continued to grow faster than my income, and on more than one occasion I had to work with my mortgage company to keep my house. *How in the world am I going to do all of this?*

But each time I thought I couldn't make it, God showed up and exceeded my expectations. In the areas of my life that I surrendered to God, he always took care of us. And as we got more involved in church, we all grew in our relationships with Christ and with each other. I could see how God was restoring what we had lost.

One wonderful friend, Cindy, always pointed me back to God—or talked me off the ledge, however you want to look at it. She reminded me of how God can redeem and restore our time, a message she had to reinforce every few months when I'd start to get anxious again. God kept telling me to be patient, and Cindy would come along to back him up.

As we talked by the pool one day, she explained how sometimes God gives us a glimpse of what is to come, but that doesn't mean he's giving us permission to take over. Oh, I was so good at taking over! Cindy encouraged me to believe that I am supposed to wait.

During this time, Richard spent a week at Allaso Ranch, our church's incredible summer camp and retreat center in east Texas. *Allaso* means "life change," and this is exactly what happens there. It is one of my favorite places in the world. Richard was a cabin leader for the high school student ministry. I loved that he did this! The only downside was that I didn't see him or talk to him for a week—there was no cell phone reception at the camp.

Allaso was a great place to hear from God. Selfishly, I was hoping that Richard would hear from God about me while he was there. The night he came back, I actually felt like maybe he had. We went to church and out to dinner. He was so sweet and attentive. At the end of the night, he pulled me close and gave me an amazing kiss. Remembering my conversation with Cindy, I reminded myself to take things one day at a time, let God lead, and enjoy the process. I couldn't know it then, but God would soon show me how making that one shift could open the way for growth in our relationship.

⊚

"Hi, Barbie. I am about to get on the plane. When we get back to Dallas tonight, would you like to meet me, Mom, and Daylee for dinner?"

Um . . . who is this? I did not expect to see Richard the day I got that call.

Not long after returning from a week at Allaso Ranch, Richard left with his family to visit extended family and enjoy the beaches in Puerto Rico. He had only called once while he was away; now not only had he called from the airport but he also texted after boarding the plane to tell me that it was great to hear my voice and that he was looking forward to seeing me. The Puerto Rican sun must have had a positive effect on him.

I love it!

I met Richard, his mom, and Daylee for dinner, and he surprised me with a dress he'd bought for me in Old San Juan. I knew that family time was precious to Richard, so his taking the time to shop for me while he was on a family trip meant so much. Getting an invitation to join all of them for dinner was like icing on the cake. I felt like he'd really missed me while he was away.

Over the next month, we saw each other frequently. We were having fun leading home team together and hanging out with his family. He took me to watch Daylee in her school play and in her dance competition, and I was falling in love with both of them. I couldn't wait to see what the holidays would be like. Richard and I had the same holiday visitation schedule with our kids during our second year of seeing each other, and I hoped it would free us up to spend some time together.

"So . . . what are you doing for Thanksgiving?" I asked him. "Neither of us have our kids this year."

Richard told me he would be visiting his mom in Lubbock, Texas. *Awesome!* I thought. *Maybe he will take me.* I had never liked being home alone when my kids were with their dads, so time away with Richard sounded like a great way to spend Thanksgiving. We had been dating, sort of, for a year and a half, and meeting more of his family over the holidays seemed appropriate.

Well, at least it did to one of us. But Richard informed me that he wanted to make the trip alone.

In the past, Richard told me, when he'd taken women home, he had to keep them entertained when all he wanted to do was hang out with his mom. It sounded like an excuse to me, but his mind was made up, and no disappointment on my part was going to change it. I was not going home with him. I felt so hurt.

Richard

It's Not Time Yet

I'm not ready for this! I don't like feeling pressured to make a decision, and I was definitely feeling pressure from Barbie. In the early years, time without Daylee at the major holidays was terrible to say the least, but by now I had gotten used to spending some holidays without her. I knew it was different for Barbie. It often is for single moms; they're used to the kids being around more often. So when the holidays roll around, they tend to feel the emptiness a little more deeply. I knew this was what Barbie was dealing with. She didn't want to be alone for Thanksgiving and feel the loneliness. While I felt bad for her, I wasn't at that point in our relationship where I felt the need to invite her to spend Thanksgiving with my family. Sure, we'd all met for dinner in Dallas. But that was different.

I was fiercely protective of my holidays with my family. We've walked through some tough times. Dad's death and my divorce had plunged me into a very dark place, and it was my family who walked me through all of it. I'd even moved in with my sister and brother-in-law at one point. So to say they are my safe place is an understatement, and I hadn't felt peace about bringing anyone new into that place for quite some time. The next time I brought someone home for the holidays, I wanted to be sure it was someone really important to me—not that Barbie wasn't, but my feelings were all over the place. I cared for her very much, but in my opinion, we weren't there yet—or at least I wasn't. And I went home without her.

Barbie

Vegas, Here I Come

A few days after getting the Thanksgiving decision from Richard, I talked to my oldest son on the phone. I guess Nate must have felt bad for me when he heard I'd be spending Thanksgiving alone. He told me that he had spoken to his dad, my first husband, and I was invited to have Thanksgiving dinner at their home in Las Vegas.

I appreciated the invitation and their offer to find me a good deal on a hotel room. It was easy for me to accept their hospitality, knowing it wouldn't be awkward spending time with them. My first husband and I were only married for three years and had since maintained a good friendship. *What the heck. This might be fun.*

As happy as I always was to spend time with Nate, I was crushed that Richard did not want to spend Thanksgiving with me. My relationship with him was such an emotional roller coaster. We were having fun leading home team, spending most weekends together and hanging out with his sister and her family. He had no real reason not to take me home with him other than he just wasn't ready. *Seriously, God? Why do you keep telling me to be patient for a man who is not interested?*

I thought I would mostly be hanging out in northern Las Vegas with Nate's family. But Nate had plans of his own and was busier than I'd thought, so I spent way too much time alone at the hotel and, never having been a gambler, inside my head about the state of my life. I decided to send an email to Richard letting him know exactly how I felt:

> *Good Morning,*
>   *I am glad you made it to Lubbock! So . . . I need to share with you. I know you have told me you are struggling. I am*

also. I am nowhere close to wanting to get married or anything like that. How I do feel is that I care about you. I want to spend time with you with an open heart and mind to what God has in store for us.

The thing is, that when I try to be open with you I feel that it is not reciprocated. You shared with me that you tell the young adults in student ministry that it takes more effort for you not to raise your hands in worship than it does to raise them. This is how the way you treat me feels. I feel like you spend a lot of time trying not to treat me the way you really want to. Like, you show kindness, compassion, and decency to all the people around you, but put a lot of effort into not showing these things to me. I don't understand, but it is painful.

I guess what I am saying is, maybe we need to be praying during this time apart. I just need to know that you can commit to having an open heart and mind, trusting me and trusting God to see where this is going. I want nothing more than to be with you. I just don't want to be convenient until what you really want comes along. That is too painful. I have to know that you are here for me. I know God is working on each one of us, but the question is, do we want to go through this process together. I hope so!

Happy Thanksgiving!

Barbie

Richard

It's Not You, It's Me

I traveled to Lubbock to relax and spend time with my family, and I got an email from Barbie that kind of turned things upside down. What was I supposed to say to her? I'd already struggled with some guilt over leaving her behind. I couldn't help but think of her alone in a Vegas hotel room and wonder if I should have invited her to my mom's to spend time with me and the family for Thanksgiving. At the same time, I didn't want to move things along faster than I was ready for.

There were struggles I was going through that I didn't expect Barbie to understand. She knew what I'd been through in my past, but she didn't really *know* what I'd been through in my past, if that makes sense. Maybe that's one of the reasons I kept my walls up. I had been single for eight years, and I'd worked hard to reach this point in my life where I was finally content with who I was in Christ—understanding my relationship with him.

Maybe this was what made it so hard to invite someone in. I was comfortable where I was, and the lack of a committed relationship had made the space I needed in order to know Christ more deeply. I liked having that time and growing in my relationship, and I didn't know how a serious relationship might affect that. But I also knew that he didn't like to leave me in a comfort zone. He wanted me to be comfortably uncomfortable, to stretch and be more. So really, the struggle was all mine, and Barbie was getting caught in the crossfire.

Barbie

Peace Beyond Understanding

I ended up having a wonderful time in Vegas. I loved spending time with my oldest! I got a chance to see that he was doing great, and I was so proud of him. It was hard to believe that he had grown into a man.

Nate and I had a fun few days when he was free. We went to the drag races and had frozen hot chocolate. I also spent some time with his girlfriend. It looked like I was not the only one falling for someone. I found myself hoping that they would take it slow. (Funny how that is good advice for someone else but not yourself.) My time with him went by too fast, and before I knew it, I was heading home wondering what the future held with Richard.

Back home from Vegas, Richard and I had a three-hour conversation. He told me that he had missed me while he was in Lubbock and that he had decided to "commit to the relationship." I wasn't exactly sure what that meant, but it gave me hope.

Fast-forward a few days. Nothing specific about our relationship seemed to have changed a lot, but things were really good between us. I think the biggest change was in me. I was finally allowing God to give me his promised "peace beyond understanding"—because now I had peace, even though nothing made any more sense than it had a few days earlier.

> *I thought after walking in obedience that God would give me what I wanted. Ha ha. What happens is that God gives us what he wants for us. This is always better than what we can imagine.*
> —Barbie's Journal

FINDING YOUR RIGHT COMBINATION

What Richard and I Learned About Restoration and Waiting

God can dream a bigger dream for you than you can dream for yourself. God is in the business of restoring lives, and he wants to redeem the years you lost.

When God was working on restoring my life, he began with working on me. God always cares most about who we become in the process. But be warned: demolition is not comfortable. We all love analogies such as a butterfly emerging from its cocoon or a house being renovated, until we are the one waiting and working through the difficulties. What I learned is that restoration is so worth the price!

Richard and I both had fears of repeating past mistakes, but Richard had a particular fear of new patterns producing the same painful results of the past. He believed that the experiences that he had before committing his life to Christ were the way it would always be. This led to a lot of the waiting we did in our relationship, and it also led to a lot of unexpected and necessary growth for both of us. If only we could have seen what God was doing behind the scenes.

God's vision for your life is bigger than you can imagine. You know the reaction people have on TV when they see their newly remodeled house? They have their hand over their mouth and tears in their eyes. That is the look you would have if you could see the life God has waiting for you. He is a loving God. You just have to trust him—even when things seem to be taking too long.

What God's Word Says About Restoration and Waiting

GOD, your God, will restore everything you lost; he'll have compassion on you; he'll come back and pick up the pieces from all the places where you were scattered. (Deuteronomy 30:3 MSG)

Lead me in Your truth and teach me, for You are the God of my salvation; on You I wait all the day. (Psalm 25:5 NKJV)

Where there is no prophetic vision the people cast off restraint. (Proverbs 29:18 ESV)

See, I am doing a new thing! Now it springs up; do you not perceive it? I am making a way in the wilderness and streams in the wasteland. (Isaiah 43:19)

As God shows you more Scriptures that relate to restoration and waiting, write them on this page too.

ೢ⊚ೢ

Psalm 27:14; Ecclesiastes 3:1, 11; Isaiah 40:30–31; 2 Corinthians 5:17

Begin Your Own Process

- In what areas of your life do you sense God wanting to do some "demo"?
- Are there any decisions you are putting off that you might need to make in order to move forward?
- If so, what is one step can you take today?

Spend some time writing your vision for your life. Pray and ask God to show you his vision for specific areas of your life. For example, your relationship with him, your relationship with each member of your family, dating and marriage, meaningful work, household finances, the church you attend or need to find, housing. Make note of any other specific areas where you feel you need vision, and write down God's answers as they become clear to you.

CHAPTER 7

You Be You and I'll Be Me

Being Authentically You

You need to be authentically who God made you to be.
—Barbie's Counselor

Barbie

I WANT TO BE WHO I AM ALL THE TIME—in person, online, and no matter who I am with. This was a decision I made one day after a friend shared some pictures she had taken from a recent trip she went on with a group of her friends. She talked about what a great time they'd had and shared the pictures that she'd posted to her social media as well as the ones she hadn't posted. Believe me, the difference was pretty drastic. The ones that had been shared were all the groups of friends hanging out, swimming, and dressed up for dinner. The ones that weren't shared, well, those were the ones that were taken after dinner and after a few drinks. I guess they were the ones deemed "inappropriate" and best left on the camera roll, to be deleted later or only used in private for a laugh between friends.

Hmm . . . God had my attention and I couldn't help taking a closer look at who I was making myself out to be. I guess that's the thing. We can be whoever we want to be on social media. We frame ourselves up in the best possible light, and that's what the world sees because that's what we want them to see. In a way, we kind of manipulate the opinions of others, and I found myself wondering if I was doing that as well.

I had to admit that I was one person at home, where I was usually found with my hair in a scrunchy and wearing my glasses as I took refuge on my front porch swing. At church, I was probably the most myself. We attend a church where jeans with heels, my look of choice, is appropriate dress. I was also making some good girlfriends with whom I was comfortable being myself. It was probably the most comfortable I had ever been being able to share my past as well as my hopes and dreams.

I was for sure another person with Richard. I spent hours in my head trying to figure out and narrow down what it would take to interest the man. On my way to a date with him one day, I went so far as to make a special stop to purchase a new pink shirt. I never wear pink. However, I had discovered that pink was Richard's favorite color. *Maybe this will help.*

I waited all through dinner and a movie for his approving comment about how nice I looked in that stinking shirt. *Not one word* came out of his mouth. I was so frustrated by his lack of response that I actually challenged him at one point by asking what he thought of my new shirt and its color. You know what he said? "Red isn't a new color for you." Really? I took the shirt back the next day. Looking back on that choice, I have to laugh at myself and wonder why in the world I ever thought wearing a pink shirt would nudge Richard over the edge and into a committed relationship. We all do crazy things sometimes to increase the odds of swinging another person's opinion in our favor, don't we?

The truth is, after my divorce, I didn't know who I was. I had spent most of my twelve-year second marriage trying to dodge the angry words of a man I just wanted to please. I put a lot of energy into being anything and everything I thought he wanted and needed so that I would earn his love and approval, and I found I was carrying this method of relating to a man into my new single life. I just didn't realize I was clinging to old patterns or that I was even in need of making a change. Trying to make a man happy was what I knew, and right or wrong, it was a comfortable place. Richard being Richard really threw that reality up on the big screen and forced me to take a long, hard look at myself. He wasn't looking for someone to be what he wanted any more than he was looking to be what someone else wanted—and boy, would God use Richard to inspire me to discover and live out my authentic self as our relationship grew!

If dealing with embracing my own true self wasn't enough, God also began taking me through the process of letting go of my old romantic notions of love by encouraging me to see and accept the authenticity of others, and again he used Richard to propel me forward.

Richard had shared many pre-Barbie stories about his addiction, recovery, failed marriage, and faith in long conversations shared on the patios of our favorite restaurants, but it wasn't until I had an opportunity to hear him speak during a church service at his treatment center that I began to see him for who he truly was. I sat and watched him, and as the words poured from him, I felt my eyes were opened for the first time to see Richard from a much deeper place. I was so moved by his powerful story and his raw honesty as he stood in front of everyone and laid himself bare. I realized that, in spite of what I thought I knew about him, the person he described before I knew him was a stranger to me. The road he'd traveled had challenged him and shaped him in ways I hadn't really understood before, and as I sat there I felt a new understanding take hold of me. For the first time, I could really see how God was doing incredible, amazing things in and through Richard. I didn't know it at the time, but God was planting the seeds in me that would grow into appreciating the importance of allowing both of us to embrace our own authenticity as well as that of others, especially those closest to us.

Richard

God Is Lifting the Veil

Barbie wasn't the only one being changed during those first couple of years of our dating. I was always quick to point out the need for her to be herself while I held her at arm's length and prevented her from really getting to know me. I didn't want her to be too close. If she was too close, she could look inside the crazy mess of my past or upset the carefully constructed walls of my present. God had grown me in many ways through my failed marriage and addiction treatment, but in the same way he used me to stretch Barbie, I was also being stretched and challenged to be real by her.

We'd had a really tough time at Thanksgiving during our second year together. Refusing to let Barbie go with me to spend time with my family was probably taking a pretty hard stance, but taking her with me seemed like such a big step—one I wasn't sure I was ready to take. I liked spending time with her, but she seemed so intent on me being "the one" that it scared me. Instead of opening up, I held back every time she wanted to talk about taking our relationship to the next level. Unconsciously, I'd close myself off to keep her at a comfortable distance. I was content in the spaces I'd defined for myself with my family, my daughter, and my faith. Comfortable is a good place from our perspective, but I've found that's right where God dumps us from our recliner and into the dirt.

Even my family had begun to question my tactics with Barbie as we sat around and talked together during the holiday. They had warned me that I needed to really think about my feelings for Barbie, that it wasn't fair to her to string her along if I did not plan to commit. They couldn't see the value in continuing to see her if I was going to end up hurting her in the end. I couldn't help but wonder if it was time to reconsider how I looked at her.

The truth was, my heart for her was softening, but still I was uneasy with the idea of jumping into a full-on committed relationship with her and opening up to the idea of marriage and blending a family. Barbie and I had had plenty of long talks about this, but I was just not there yet, and up until the Thanksgiving visit alone with my family, I was afraid of where it might take me to confess that I did have feelings for her that might just take us into the future. But I couldn't ignore the truth in what they'd had to say on the subject. I gave my family's thoughts some long hard consideration and decided that when I returned home, I wanted to be willing to let Barbie see more of me. What I realized was, I had closed myself off for so long not out of a need for protection but more from a need for spiritual growth. Now I was mature in my walk with Christ, content in who I was, but I was still acting as if I needed protection or more spiritual growth before I could move deeper into my relationship with Barbie. All I really needed was to let go, trust God, and let Barbie in closer to my and Daylee's life.

So when I got back in town, I called Barbie and invited her over. We sat in the living room of my apartment, as we had on many occasions to discuss and communicate our feelings, and I shared with her what I was dealing with and how I knew it wasn't fair to her. I told her I didn't feel good about my choice to not let her come to Thanksgiving, and I wanted to be more committed to our relationship. I could tell Barbie was happy to hear what I was saying, and I was glad not just to see how much she cared but also to realize someone who wasn't my family cared so much for me.

My concerns weren't just for me or for Barbie. What about our kids? Too many people jump from one relationship to the next hoping to fulfill whatever they feel is missing in their life, only to find that next person is not the answer, and it confused me to see people with children jump into relationships. Maybe they thought their kids needed a father figure or a mother figure in their lives. But in reality, their actions had nothing to do with the kids and everything to do with those parents getting their own needs met. I knew all too well what that was like. In the first few years of my divorce, in my arguments with my ex over weekend time, vacation time, things going on at one another's house—disagreements typical between divorced parents—I came to realize something about myself, and it wasn't pretty. No matter what the argument was about, I always said I was doing what I was doing for Daylee's sake. But in reality, I was invoking Daylee's name in support of things that were almost all about me.

After one of these arguments while returning Daylee from a visit,

I slammed the front door so hard on the way out that the windows rattled. As I hopped in my car, I heard God ask me, "What are you doing?" Right then I knew I had made a mistake. Using my daughter to justify my personal choices was wrong for Daylee and wrong for me. I promised myself that day that I would stop. I surrendered the situation to God and determined not to use Daylee as a weapon in an argument ever again. It took me a long time to get to this point in my relationship with God, trusting him and surrendering to him, but every decision was, and still is, growth in my walk.

That's why seeing others put their needs before their kids' needs hurt. I knew those parents were just using their kids selfishly to get what they wanted. And most of the time, what the parents wanted was nowhere near where God would lead them if they stopped to ask his will.

So, looking back on my relationship with Barbie in those early years, I understand how she thought I was being hardheaded with some of my decisions—and maybe I was being a little difficult. But I was also trying to focus on the bigger picture. That picture didn't just include Barbie—it included her kids as well, and of course my daughter. I thought of Daylee and of Barbie's boys, and I knew I was not ready to move toward marriage until I was ready to give all of them my best.

Barbie and I had an honest conversation when once again I felt the pressure of her wanting more of a commitment from me. I told her, "Look, I like what we have right now, but if you push this anymore and I feel like you or your boys are coming in between what me and my daughter have together, then I will resent you and resent your boys. I don't want that. Let's take our time and really get to know one another. Let me really get to know your boys, because if I cannot go into this relationship loving your boys 100 percent as if they were my own, then what I am doing is wrong." It was a great conversation that opened the door to a deeper relationship with Barbie, a relationship where I became willing to share more of myself, what I've been through, and how I see things.

Barbie

Happy New Year

When Richard returned from his solo Thanksgiving visit with his family, no one was more surprised than I was when he came to me and shared that maybe he needed to commit a little more to our relationship. It was the beginning of his trusting me enough to pull back another layer and reveal himself in a way I hadn't known him before. We were both growing, and it would open up new levels of intimacy between us. Over the next couple of years, we continued to jump over hurdles and trusted ourselves to be increasingly more real, even when it was difficult.

What I loved about our journey to authenticity was that once we crossed over a rough place, we'd have an amazing connection that would bring us a little further along. God doesn't waste the hard things. Not long after my huge disappointment at Thanksgiving, Richard invited me to join him on a road trip to visit his brother, Ralph, to celebrate the New Year. We were once again without our kids, and the prospect of spending time one-on-one during the five-hour drive made me super excited, not to mention the chance of getting to know more of Richard's family. I couldn't wait.

What a difference it was from Thanksgiving! We had so much fun. On New Year's Eve, we went out dancing with Ralph and his girlfriend. We had the best time together. I always enjoyed dancing with Richard; he's so much fun when he's dancing, and he knew how to make a girl feel like the center of his world. But the highlight of the night was when we got back to the house. We were enjoying the breakfast and the mimosas Ralph made for us when I heard Lionel Richie come on the radio. Richard immediately began dancing with me in the living room and singing in my ear. The night was so romantic, and I didn't want it to end. This was a part of Richard he hadn't let me see much of, and I liked this romantic side of him for sure.

Richard

Oddball

Barbie and I both experienced some interesting challenges to our authenticity as a couple. Not only did we have our hands full dealing with our personal baggage and the struggle to raise ourselves up, but just about everyone in our inner circles of friends and family raised an eyebrow when they found out we weren't having sex after almost two years of dating. And when we got the opportunity to share our story with singles groups at church, you can imagine how acquaintances and strangers reacted.

In some ways, it was easier on me than it was on Barbie, because I'd already been walking this road of abstinence for several years. What made it hard on me at this point as opposed to earlier times was that I now had a steady girlfriend. People take for granted that it's easier to forgo sex when you don't have a partner to tempt you. Dating Barbie for as long as I had made it really hard for anyone else to believe that we might actually be saving ourselves for marriage. Neither of us knew anyone else, especially among our divorced friends, who even considered this aspect of dating God's way important, if they considered it at all.

Since Barbie is an overthinker, the doubt that would rise up when other people questioned my intentions toward her or a possible long-term future would regularly throw her into tailspins. So many of our friends seemed to think sex was what bonded couples together in a relationship. But I'd come to see how people used it, as I did in the past, to fill an emptiness or need for validation in themselves when, in reality, they were expecting someone or something to fill a void that only God could fill.

I understood where Barbie might be confused. She wasn't receiving something that used to be part of her past relationships, and she was getting mixed signals from friends who had never surrendered this part of their life to God. All I could do was continue to reassure her how much I cared for her. I often came up short with verbalizing my feelings, but I did my best. And since I think I communicate better in writing, I sometimes also sent her notes and cards. I worked hard to understand how difficult it was for her to come alongside me and trust me as I asked her to live out life in a way that was completely the opposite of any other singles we knew, even our Christian friends.

This whole experience is best summed up by the story of a time when our church hosted a huge singles event. There must have be at least four hundred single men and women there that night. We were talking about the importance of purity and dating God's way—no sex until marriage. Our pastor pointed out that because we're not to have sex outside of marriage, the world might look at us like we're the oddball. I distinctly remember looking around the room and thinking, *Really?* There was another pastor standing next to me, and I turned to him and said, "You know what, pastor? I'm standing in a room full of Christians, and yet I still feel like I'm the oddball."

So yeah, some people talk the talk, but they don't walk the walk. I knew what it was like to walk out dating God's way, because I'd been doing it for quite some time. I was asking Barbie to take this journey with me, and I understood why she would have doubts. I hoped that by allowing her to see more of me and to be more a part of my life every day, she might have hope for the future.

Barbie

Attitude of Gratitude

"Barbie, you need to be authentically who God made you to be."

Thank goodness for the advice of my counselor. He reeled me in when I was losing it, and he gave me great perspective about what makes me tick. He told me I had a tendency to analyze and overthink everything (a fact I already knew), and while it sometimes made me crazy, that characteristic was an important part of what made me me. He encouraged me not to change, because it was those moments of insecurity that kept me dependent on God and enabled me to feel gratitude in the good times. He also suggested that I needed to learn to receive love from both God and Richard in the way each of them gave it—to believe their love was real and trustworthy. It was a tall order, but I sure wasn't staying in a good place trying to figure it out on my own.

> *I am trying to take my counselor's advice and be my authentic*
> *self, to believe that who I am is good enough, and that someone*
> *will love me the way I am. That is SO hard! How do I let go*
> *of whether or not Richard thinks I am good enough for him?*
> —Barbie's Journal

FINDING YOUR RIGHT COMBINATION

What Richard and I Learned About Being Authentic

I don't think I ever even knew for sure exactly what it means to be authentic. Who am I authentically? I had to learn to know and love myself before anyone else could know and love me.

As I began my self-discovery, I soon found that my past left clues. I thought back to what I liked to do as a kid. I asked myself questions like, *What am I passionate about? What colors do I actually like to wear?* When I stopped trying so hard to be someone I wasn't, I found that it took less effort to be myself. It's exhausting trying to be everything to everyone.

Being authentic begins with knowing who you are in Christ. If you aren't confident in who you are, you might take on someone else's image, especially in dating. *Oh, he likes baseball? I can do that.* If you don't really enjoy it as well, though, doing what he loves will be fun for a while, but you might grow to resent how for him, date night looks like going to a ball game. Then you hear, "But I thought you enjoyed it!"

A vital part of authenticity is about each of you knowing who you are and sharing your interests.

When Richard was newly divorced and after he had gotten back from treatment, often after taking Daylee back to her mom's from a visit, he would return to his apartment, shut the door, and sit on his sofa in silence. It was so quiet that he'd yell at the top of his lungs, "I'm so lonely I don't even know who I am anymore."

God began to show Richard that his Word was true and that Richard was perfectly and wonderfully made in God's image. Being who God made him to be was something to be proud of, not embarrassed about. Richard is authentically loud and has never been accused of having an indoor voice. He is goofy, fun loving, and will say things others won't say. That is who he is. Once he got back to loving himself, he realized that is who God wanted him to be all the time. He wanted Richard to accept himself as God's perfect creation.

Now it's your turn. Spend some time discovering who you are authentically. You are awesome! When you begin to see and appreciate your own uniqueness, others will begin to see it as well. Freedom is found in authenticity—in being who God created you to be. Life is too short to live it as a people pleaser. God made you uniquely perfect, so let us see *you*. Following are some Scriptures and prompts to jump-start your journey toward being more fully yourself.

What God's Word Says About Being Authentically You

Do not conform to the pattern of this world, but be transformed by the renewing of your mind. Then you will be able to test and approve what God's will is—his good, pleasing and perfect will. (Romans 12:2)

If anyone is in Christ, he is a new creation. The old has passed away; behold, the new has come. (2 Corinthians 5:17 ESV)

Am I now trying to win the approval of human beings, or of God? Or am I trying to please people? If I were still trying to please people, I would not be a servant of Christ. (Galatians 1:10)

We are God's handiwork, created in Christ Jesus to do good works, which God prepared in advance for us to do. (Ephesians 2:10)

As God shows you more Scriptures that relate to being authentically you, write them on this page too.

൭◉൭

John 8:32; Romans 8:29–30; 12:9; 1 Corinthians 12:12–31; Ephesians 1:11–14

Begin Your Own Process

Discovering who God made you to be takes courage to be willing to really see yourself, and it can be so fun!

- What hobbies did you enjoy as a kid, teen, or young adult? Do you still do this? Why or why not?
- Be alert to words that set you apart as a unique individual. Use the following sentence to try out different words: "I believe the very essence of my name, _____, is _____ (words that describe you)."
- Values are who we are. Not who we think we would like to be, not who we think we should be, but who we really are in our lives right now. Identifying your values will help you live more consistently with your true identity. What words would you use to describe your core values?

When we operate our life personally and professionally within our values, we come alive and find our energy. When we are not in alignment with our values, our life can feel draining and unfulfilling. Values show us what is important. When we are clear on what we value, it is easier to recognize when the person we are dating doesn't line up with who we are.

It's vital to be honest with what is important to us before we can even hope to take the first steps toward wholeness. If we can't be honest with ourselves first, how can we ever be authentic with the other people in our life?

CHAPTER 8

The Walls Come Down

Being Vulnerable

*I am stepping out in faith and putting my heart on
the line. God, please let this be for real.*
—Barbie's Journal

Richard

THE NEW YEAR OPENED ON A GREAT NOTE. I had a wonderful
weekend spending time with Barbie, my brother, and his girlfriend. As
with every year, time flew by so fast and brought with it more change.
The lease on my apartment was coming up for renewal, and I had been
thinking I'd really like to move. After living in those apartments for four
years, I was ready for a change of scenery.

I had recently spoken to a friend of mine about the opportunity to
move into a house he knew might be coming open, but since it never
came through, I knew I had to make another plan.

One day as I was working out in the gym, I was praying to God
over a solution to my housing problem. I had become so much better at
placing even the little decisions I made in his hands and trusting that he
would lead me to the best answers. *Lord, what is my next move? I feel like
I'm going to be moving, and I would really like a change.*

I'm not kidding—within seconds of praying that prayer, I received a text message from a friend who attended my church: "How would you like to live in an apartment free of rent and do ministry work?"

Seriously? "Yes, tell me more!"

We jumped on the phone right away, and he began telling me about this ministry called Apartment Life. It sounded like an amazing opportunity for me to save money on my living expenses and share God with others. But what about my daughter? If she couldn't come on my weekend with her, then it was a no-go. He checked into it and got right back with me. Sure enough, they said it was no problem to arrange for us to have a three-bedroom apartment. I told him, "I'm in. Let's do this!"

Best-Laid Plans

The next time Barbie and I were together, I shared my decision to take the apartment ministry position. But even though it seemed an answer to my prayer, she was visibly upset. I knew right away I'd caught her off guard. Heck, the opportunity caught *me* off guard, but I really felt God had opened this door. I believed he was calling me to be in ministry, and I was already leading in student ministry and in singles ministry at my church. Taking the apartment post seemed like another natural step toward that future.

The problem was, I hadn't taken Barbie's opinion into account before I committed to the job. After all, committing to do apartment ministry meant that I was agreeing to live in an apartment with my friend Ben for two years. Suddenly I felt terrible. I'd already made life difficult by building walls to keep her from getting too close, and now I'd made this decision without considering its impact on her, let alone discussing it with her. Having lived as a single dad for so long, it never occurred to me to ask her thoughts. From Barbie's standpoint, I was asking her—without ever *really* asking her—to hang on at least two more years for something to come of our relationship.

When the move into the apartment came, right off the bat my faith was tested—but not by Barbie. The apartment complex I was assigned to live in was not in the best part of town, and my ex-wife and Daylee's stepdad were concerned that it was not safe enough for our daughter. Apparently I had overlooked a couple of important aspects of accepting the assignment, and it could have affected my visitation rights. Thankfully, it didn't. I was able to work through the matter, and I was free to have my daughter visit me at my new location.

Barbie

What About Me?

I knew Richard was having a difficult enough time maneuvering things with Daylee and her mom, but I couldn't help but be surprised that he'd make such a big commitment without even thinking to discuss it with me. He didn't need my permission, but the oversight of even talking to me about it just reinforced the insecurities I already felt surrounding my place in his life. Here I was trying to really open up and be vulnerable, and now this. We had been dating almost exactly two years, and this apartment ministry was for a two-year period. I didn't want him to do it because it would only delay for that much longer any long-term commitment he might make to me. *What about me? Doesn't what I think matter?*

The one thing I could not argue with was the feeling that God had brought him this opportunity. But what did it mean for me? We still had not talked about marriage, and he was not promising that at the end of the two-year ministry we would get married. I couldn't help wondering if I would ever mean as much to Richard as he meant to me.

Once, as I was confiding to a girlfriend about how long it was taking for Richard to come around, she shared an amazing insight that encouraged me to continue to hope. "What I hear is pride," she said. "You want what you want when you want it, and you are not thinking about how God is working on Richard." This was hard to hear; the truth always is. But I was so grateful for a friend who spoke the truth in love. God *was* working in Richard's life, and I knew he would do amazing things during his time in the apartments. I decided that all I could do was be supportive and pray—and keep waiting. But I almost quit before the journey really began.

The first time that Richard and his ministry partner, Ben, were scheduled to hold an event for his new apartment ministry, I had agreed to go over and help them out. I needed Richard to provide me with an address because I didn't know where I was going. I knew the apartment was in Dallas since I had been there once, but I didn't remember exactly how to get there. He'd promised to send me the information, but I'd been waiting since the night before to hear from him.

Since I knew the general area where I would be going, I got up early on that Saturday morning and headed toward Dallas, still waiting for something from Richard. By this point, I had texted and called him several times with no response. His silence felt like another rejection, and I was sad and hurt. *After all this time, why doesn't he ever think of me?*

At some point it hit me: I had had enough. This was just too hard. I was so tired of not being thought of by him; all too often our relationship felt so one-sided. I had been trying to be more transparent and be more me, but he was not letting me in, and I was losing hope that he ever would. Still waiting to know where I was headed, I pulled into a parking lot and called my friend Cindy. She was always Richard's biggest supporter, and she encouraged me as I waited by telling me that God would redeem my time. I needed her to boost me, but that day when I spoke to her even she was different. As I shared my hurt and disappointment with her, she felt compelled to agree with me.

I cannot do this anymore.

I concluded that I needed to tell him we were over. I drove to a park and sat with my Bible and journal to contemplate and pray. This was taking my desire to be vulnerable to another level. Now I was really going to have to open up and tell him how I felt. *Am I really ready to risk not having him in my life?*

While sitting there, the sound of a text interrupted my thoughts. It was a message from another girlfriend I had not heard from in a long time. She said, "I am thinking of you right now and praying for you." I knew right then that I was not alone, that God was with me. I asked her what prompted her to text, and she said she felt God had brought me to mind as she was praying. *I am so grateful for praying friends!*

I continued journaling, and eventually Richard called. I told him how hurt I felt over being forgotten once again, but I knew he was busy with his ministry event, and we agreed to talk later that day.

In the meantime, I had previously committed to helping Richard with Daylee's birthday party that same afternoon at Richard's ex-wife's house. I was in no mood to go and pretend that everything was okay, but I also didn't want to disappoint Daylee by not showing up for her special day. I went, but it was awkward and uncomfortable acting like it was just a normal day when it wasn't. I just couldn't get out of there fast enough.

After the party, Richard and I went back to his apartment to talk. We sat on his couch and I shared how I was feeling frustrated and hurt from that morning, not to mention all the other times that he had made me feel like I wasn't a priority. I finally got the courage to share with him that I just couldn't do our relationship this way any longer.

As if he'd known what I was going to say, he said, "I was just telling my brother that I am not giving you the best part of me, and that I have not really committed to the relationship." He apologized and promised that he was going to fully submit to us and our relationship. For the first time, we prayed together and prayed over our relationship. I had never had that experience with a man before. I was still unsure whether I could trust him since I had been told things I wanted to hear in my past. But I wanted to believe we'd turned a corner.

The rest of that day and the next, things were very different between us. Richard acted as though a weight had been lifted from him, and suddenly there were no more walls. He was more relaxed, fun, and flirty. I continued to feel nervous that the change was not real, but thankfully I was wrong.

Things with Richard continued to get better, and we kept growing closer. He even held my hand at church, and finally we started acting like a couple. The only explanation I had for the change was God. Only God could make walls come down in such a dramatic way, and I was so grateful. The most amazing part was how I saw our relationship pointing me back to God and reinforcing how much he loved me.

Richard

"She's Not Seeing the Best of You"

I had just spent a weekend with my brother and his girlfriend, and she'd made a comment that she didn't think I was the same person with Barbie that she saw in me. I was confused by her observation and asked her what she meant by it.

"Well," she said, "when you talk about your relationship with Barbie, you're always analyzing it. The Richard I know doesn't spend time analyzing every situation. The Richard I know is carefree, fun loving, extremely funny, and just goes with the flow. Do you think that's what Barbie sees?"

Hmm, probably not.

"If she's not seeing the Richard I see, then she's not seeing the best of you," she continued.

I couldn't put up much of an argument. She was totally right, and I started thinking that maybe it was time to let down the walls and let Barbie inside. Maybe I'd taken this protection thing too far. After all, we had been dating for more than two years.

You know, I once heard that if you walk around with walls up to protect yourself, yeah, you protect yourself, but what you don't realize is you also stop love from coming inside.

Barbie

"I Do Love You, Babe"

"I do love you, babe."

What?

It was a couple months after our last landmark conversation. We were sitting in the car in front of Richard's apartment, saying good night at the end of a date. He was hugging me—and then he told me the words I had waited so long to hear.

I found it so hard to believe, I had to ask him to repeat himself to make sure I'd heard him correctly.

Sometimes when you've prayed for something so long, it is hard to believe when it actually does happen. I am so grateful for a good Father who wants to give us the desires of our heart.

> *It is so crazy, today Richard was completely different! It was as if a wall had come down. He was so playful and flirty. Only God could make that kind of overnight change.*
> —Barbie's Journal

FINDING YOUR RIGHT COMBINATION

What Richard and I Learned About Being Vulnerable

I believe we all have a desire to be seen, to be known, and to be loved. But allowing that to happen takes vulnerability and feels like risk. I always thought it was Richard who was not being vulnerable, but it was also me. I tried to be who I thought I needed to be to get his attention. That day in Richard's apartment, when I told him I couldn't continue in our relationship the way it was, I finally let him see the real me and my real needs at the risk that he would let me go.

Richard has shared with me since that he wanted to be with me but didn't want to change how things had always been with him and Daylee. His brother and his girlfriend helped him see that he would have to risk vulnerability or else possibly lose me. When Richard's walls came down, I myself was forced to a new level of transparency I wasn't used to. At some point you have to let others see who you are, inside and out.

I still believe that what made the real difference for us was prayer. From my perspective, when Richard and I prayed together, I saw the change in Richard. We do not always get instant results; I had personally been praying for Richard's walls to come down for two years. We have to remember that we cannot accomplish anything by our own strength. When we do what we can do, God will do what only he can do.

Being vulnerable is one of the bravest things we can do. If we have been through a divorce, it can be difficult to allow ourselves to risk again. When we keep our walls up to protect ourselves from getting hurt, we also keep out the love that others want to give.

Let others see who you are. You've got this!

What God's Word Says About Being Vulnerable

And I will give you a new heart, and a new spirit I will put within you. And I will remove the heart of stone from your flesh and give you a heart of flesh. (Ezekiel 36:26 ESV)

[God] said to me, "My grace is sufficient for you, for my power is made perfect in weakness." Therefore I will boast all the more gladly about my weaknesses, so that Christ's power may rest on me. That is why, for Christ's sake, I delight in weaknesses, in insults, in hardships, in persecutions, in difficulties. For when I am weak, then I am strong. (2 Corinthians 12:9–10)

We are God's handiwork, created in Christ Jesus to do good works, which God prepared in advance for us to do. (Ephesians 2:10)

Confess your sins to each other and pray for each other so that you may be healed. The prayer of a righteous person is powerful and effective. (James 5:16)

As God shows you more Scriptures that relate to being vulnerable, write them on this page too.

෧◉෧

Proverbs 12:22; John 13:34–35; Philippians 4:13; Colossians 3:9–10;
1 Thessalonians 5:21

Begin Your Own Process

Taking a chance and risking vulnerability can take some practice. It can be difficult, but it is not nearly as hard as living a life running from real love and acceptance.

- Are you allowing yourself to really be known by other people? If yes, in what ways? If not, what is holding you back?
- Do you believe you deserve to be loved for who you are? If yes, in whom or what are you finding your value? If not, what lies are you holding on to about yourself?
- What is one step you can take today toward vulnerability in your life?

You have a unique and special something to share with the world. You are worthy! The way you look, the way you laugh, the way you sing and dance when nobody's watching. Choose someone in your life—a friend, a family member, or someone you're interested in—and make a decision to allow them to see the real you. Consider what steps you can take to make that happen, and then start taking them.

CHAPTER 9

Comfortably Uncomfortable

Moving Out of Your Comfort Zone

When God allows you to see more, he empowers you to do more.
—Richard

Barbie

THE HOLIDAYS ALWAYS SEEMED TO MARK CHANGE for us, and what a difference a year could make. Richard and I had circled around to our third Thanksgiving together, and oh my gosh, how far we'd come! For the first time, the boys and I planned to spend the holiday with Richard and Daylee, and after three days together with the entire Armenta family, I had fallen completely in love with Richard and Daylee. I felt blessed beyond measure.

Our time together didn't come without challenges. Richard and I were still learning how to maneuver the dynamics of merging the traditions and expectations of all the people involved, and I usually didn't know the best way to handle the communications. When I tried, I ended up feeling like I was getting it all wrong. I wanted to be with my boys, of course, but I also wanted to see Richard, and Richard wanted to be with both me and his family. It sometimes felt like a monumental task to pull it all together and make everyone happy. Coming together with new people at our house, or with other family members at their homes, always changed "the way things have always been" and stretched us to consider compromises and setting new traditions. We often felt like it was a no-win situation. All of it was way out of my comfort zone for sure. But, as my pastor says, sometimes you have to learn to get comfortably uncomfortable.

When you think about blending families, you usually think about yourself and the kids. I had never given much thought to extended family or how we would make it all work. For Richard's family, it had just been Richard and Daylee for so long that adding me and two or three boys could make it feel like a crowd in a hurry. It was clearly going to be an adjustment for everyone. I was beginning to understand why a huge percentage of second marriages end in divorce. If a couple did not address all the seemingly small issues while dating, I could only imagine the struggle after the wedding.

Richard

What's Yours Is Yours, and What's Mine Is Mine

Now that I'd let my walls come down, I was really starting to enjoy my time with Barbie and the boys. We had always done some things together, but now we were participating in more events that included all the kids— her boys and my daughter—along with extended family.

However, I was finding out really fast that blending families was not an easy task. Barbie felt like everyone had to be included in everything we did, but I didn't feel the same way. Our differences created many disagreements between the two of us as well as between me and my family. Not everyone saw the blended family the same way, especially the extended family members.

Planning family gatherings could get ugly sometimes. Early on, I understood that if Barbie was the person I truly thought I wanted to spend my life with, then I needed to act that way. It wasn't easy because I was having to choose between two good things, and I knew that no matter what choice I made, someone's feelings would be hurt. But I finally made a choice to support, defend, and stand behind my possible future family. That meant I made sure we included everyone in all we were doing, to the best of my ability.

Barbie

Moving Out of the Comfort Zone

"Someone from Fellowship Church called, and they want to interview you for a job."

What? I was so confused. My boss at the salon was telling me that someone at my church wanted to interview me. I wondered, *Are you firing me?* But he said he knew how important the church was to me and thought I would want to know.

I loved my current job working for the best salon in the Dallas area, and I loved being a part of their team. I couldn't help but be intrigued, however, with the thought of working in ministry. My faith had become such a big part of my life over the past few years, and the thought of working every day at my church was hugely attractive. I was curious to check out the offer.

Over the next two weeks, I was swept up in a whirlwind of change I never saw coming. Suddenly I was being offered a position with my church, and I was saying goodbye to my career in the beauty industry and hello to a new one in ministry. I was amazed at the ways I continued to see God at work in my life, and I had to admit he did a much better job orchestrating my life than I did. I was also so grateful for the support I received from Richard as I was making this decision. We had come so far from him feeling that this was "his" church, to the two of us serving together, and now to my actually working at the church. God was doing so much more than I ever could have asked or imagined. I never dreamed, back when I sat in the newcomer's class, that I would one day be on staff at Fellowship Church.

The day I was supposed to start my new job, we had a crazy snow-storm, and everything in the Dallas/Fort Worth area shut down. Texans are notoriously unprepared for this kind of weather, so we were stuck at home for the next three days. I spent the first day worried that I should be at work instead of enjoying my day off. The second morning, my new supervisor called and told me to continue enjoying my time in between. Wow! I was suddenly struck with an understanding that I had been sitting at home stressing over something that was completely out of my control when God knew all along I wouldn't be starting my new job yet. I realized I was blessed to have a few days of rest with my boys, and I just needed to change my perspective. We had so much fun. We enjoyed making snowballs and sitting by a warm fire, days that Michael and Dalton would later remember as "the Crock Pot days." They would come in from playing in the snow to the smell of yet another meal in the Crock Pot. I saw not having to go to the store as a blessing.

Michael was determined to ride his bike on the ice up to the convenience store. Dalton and I stood in the garage and laughed our heads off as he struggled to make it down the driveway. He did manage to get there and back with a movie, chips, and some other snacks. That time in between jobs was such a good time, and we made so many memories, just the three of us.

I got a card from Richard while I was waiting to start my new job. Dayspring e-cards seemed to be his love language. Whenever he and I had serious conversations or something was bothering me, Richard would send me the sweetest e-cards to cheer me up or let me know he was thinking of me. These little things only made me fall even more completely in love with him.

Galveston, Here We Come

Before we knew it, summer had arrived and the boys were out of school. I had been looking forward to taking them on a long weekend trip to the beach and trying to convince Richard to come along. I was so excited the day Richard finally decided he would go to Galveston with us. It took him weeks to finally say yes. I was not sure what made him join us, but I couldn't have been happier.

Right on the heels of my happiness over having him join us, I began to get nervous. One aspect of blending families was in realizing that what is normal to one family can be completely opposite of how the other family does things. For example, when the boys and I took road trips, we made stops if we got hungry, needed a bathroom break, or just saw something interesting. Richard, on the other hand, was destination oriented. When he hit the road, he might stop for a quick bite or bathroom break, but that was it.

This time, on one of our unplanned stops heading to Galveston, Dalton, my eleven-year-old, realized he did not have his shoes. *Holy cow!* Dalton commonly took his shoes off when he was in the car, but this time he just didn't bring them at all. Worse yet, he hadn't packed any either. So we had to make yet another stop at a shoe store. I was so worried that Richard was going to be frustrated, and I'm sure he was. But he never showed it. He was so sweet with the whole process, proving to me once again what a good man I'd found.

Once in Galveston, we were back on track. Richard and I started each morning with a walk on the beach, and in the afternoons we would catch the boys learning to ride the skim boards we'd brought along. We were all having so much fun.

As excited as I was for Richard to be with me, I quickly realized that his being there had much more to do with building his relationship with my boys than it would ever benefit the two of us. They loved being together. But the most telling moment was at the end of our first day. We had collected our towels and skim boards and headed back to the car. The boys stopped behind the car wondering what to do with their boards since they were covered in sand. "Just throw them in the trunk," Richard told them. The boys looked at each other and back at Richard. "But they are covered in sand," Michael said. Richard assured them that was of no concern to him. So they loaded up the trunk, and we all hopped in the car to head back to our condo.

This might have seemed like a normal exchange to most people, but for my boys and me, it was a defining moment. We were not used to a man with such a relaxed attitude about getting the car dirty, and Richard's ease was a nice surprise. It set the tone for the rest of our trip.

We enjoyed fun times on the beach, music on the pier, and fabulous breakfasts at a one-hundred-year-old restaurant. Our little getaway had turned into one of the most memorable and joyful times we'd had in a long time.

On the third night of our trip, Richard put the icing on the cake. He and I were sitting out on a jetty watching some guys shark fish when, out of nowhere, Richard looked at me and said, "You won me over. I do want to marry you."

Richard

The Almost-Family That Travels Together Stays Together

I had to think long and hard before accepting Barbie's invitation to join her and the boys for a Galveston road trip weekend. We'd never traveled with her kids, and I wasn't sure if I was ready. It would just be me. Daylee was with her mom and wouldn't be joining us. I was hesitant at first but then realized if we were going to truly explore the idea of becoming a family, then I needed to be all in. Not to mention, taking this trip together would give me a good idea of the true temperature of things between all of us. You know how trips can be; they can either show the best or the worst of someone—usually the latter. So I decided to go to see how we all got along in a new environment. Besides, I love the ocean, and I thought it would be a blast to introduce the boys to skim boarding and snorkeling.

The day we left for Galveston was a real eye-opener. Daylee and I had always been point A to point B travelers. Not Barbie and the crew.

They loved to make stops, see things, and have little adventures along the way. A long stop at Buc-ee's and the escapade with the left-behind shoes would have normally frustrated me to no end, but we all got a good laugh out of it. It was a good road trip icebreaker, and the rest of the drive went smoothly until we got to our hotel and realized it did not exactly live up to the online pictures. We weren't in any position to change where we were staying, so we decided to make the best of a bad situation. We had one room with two beds, and we added a cot. I got a bed to myself, Barbie and Dalton shared a bed, and Michael got the cot.

When the next morning rolled around, I woke up and my legs and toes had bites all over them. *Wow! This trip is starting off with a bang.* There were bedbugs in my bed. It would have been easy to let this derail me, but I was determined to make the best of this trip. We worked out a solution with the management and went on with our day.

Barbie and I really enjoyed our time together and with the boys. It felt good to finally be myself with them, to be the carefree and fun-loving guy I hadn't always shared with Barbie or the kids. It was good for all of us. I think the little exchange between me and the boys over the sand in the car was a real game-changer for our relationship also. That one little exchange with them showed me how much they needed the example of a man who would lead with kindness and love, and it made me want to be there for them. Being with Barbie and the boys opened my eyes to how much I really did love Barbie and revealed to me just how much they all enjoyed feeling like they had a man in the family again.

Barbie

Moving On

I was sitting on my porch swing for one of the last times, remembering how good life had been for me and my boys at our home in Savannah. In just a few weeks, we would be saying goodbye to our life here. I had never been as sad and as excited all at the same time.

Savannah had been a special place for the boys and me for many reasons. I had especially felt such a sense of pride and accomplishment buying our home and providing a fresh start for my family all on my own. I never thought I could do that as a single mom, but God was always so good to provide us everything we needed and more. We were comforted and supported through many difficult times by our wonderful neighbors, who became like family to us over time. We had tons of fun, and piece by piece, we rebuilt our life there. I will always be so grateful for the few years we spent planted in that neighborhood.

As hard as it was for me to leave, it was just as difficult for the boys. We had bonded with Doug and Amy, the amazing couple who lived across the street, and from the beginning, they were always there for anything we needed. Amy and I shared many porch conversations and spent time with the kids at the pool; Amy even pet-sat our corn snake while we were away one weekend. And Doug was always so great with the boys. When Michael was starting the eighth grade, I had saved up to purchase his first laptop. But I knew nothing about how to use it, so Doug helped him set it up and showed him how it worked. Our relationship with this couple was priceless.

When we left, I offered them my favorite item from our house—my porch swing. I had spent many hours in it swinging, sipping coffee, journaling, reading my Bible, or just watching the kids play. They accepted it, and I was so happy. I knew it was going to a good home.

Sad as I was to move away, I was also excited to see what God had in store for us next. Since Richard had expressed his intent to get married, I was considering what would be best for all of us, not just the boys and me. Richard would never want to live as far out as Savannah, and I myself was struggling with the cost. Gas and toll road expenses had gotten to be too much; moving closer to the church in Dallas seemed like the best option. So I had decided to lease a place, but I had no idea where or how to start looking. I also hated having to move the boys to a new school. But I had to do what I had to do.

It wasn't long after I'd made my decision to leave Savannah that I heard through some friends at church that a couple from our campus was being transferred from the Fellowship Church campus in Grapevine, Texas, to the church's Florida campus. I was surprised, because only a few weeks prior I had attended a housewarming party at their beautiful new house in Lantana, Texas. I quickly contacted the husband, Justin, to find out what they planned to do with their house. He told me they'd be renting it out until they determined if the move to Florida was permanent. *Perfect!* I knew I needed to sell my house; I knew I needed to move closer to work; and like Justin and his wife, I didn't want to make any permanent arrangement. Renting their house sounded like it could be just the right choice. Once again, I couldn't help feeling that God was orchestrating a perfect solution.

Though it was hard to leave Savannah, the move to Lantana went smoothly. Richard and our friends from our church home team were such a big help. One blessing of the move was that Richard started coming to our house more often. He had rarely come to Savannah since it was such a far drive, and there wasn't much to do there. It was kind of different and kind of awesome to have him hanging out at the house with us. I found I was no longer able to compartmentalize my life—or maybe I was choosing not to. God was bringing all the pieces together.

Richard

Everyone's Learning

My relationship with Barbie seemed to be right where God wanted it. And while she and the boys were experiencing a huge life change in moving from way out in Savannah to closer in Lantana, I was amazed to see how God was moving in my own life as well.

My apartment ministry couldn't have been going any better. The neighborhood where Ben and I did our apartment ministry was a little rougher than I had expected, but we were making some great connections.

We served the community by cooking breakfasts in the clubhouse on Saturdays, handing out coffee and donuts in the mornings to people as they left the apartments on their way to work, and hosting cookouts by the pool once in a while. I'd even met some students at the complex and started taking them with me to attend our student ministry events.

Daylee, Barbie, her boys, and I were really enjoying our times together, and every day I could see more clearly why God had brought us all together. I felt honored that I was getting to show Barbie and the boys what a man of God looked like.

I was so happy I had taken my time to get to know Barbie and her boys. If I had jumped right into a committed relationship, I'm afraid I would have bailed out a long time ago. Every day I realized more and more what a commitment it was going to be to blend a family. Why anyone would take it lightly, or not even think about it, before rushing into a new relationship is beyond me.

Barbie

Be Still

Life in our new rental home had its ups and downs for the boys and me. I was homesick for Savannah—I missed my house, my friends, my swing, and my security. And it really didn't take less time to get to work and school. I actually had to backtrack to get to one school and then go to the other. *I knew it! Here we go.*

So many other things also seemed to come to an end at the same time. I was no longer leading home team, I didn't have my women's group anymore, and my position at work changed. I spent the first couple weeks after the move wondering whose life I was living. I didn't just leave my comfort zone—I couldn't even see it from here.

However, I know God doesn't waste anything, and it didn't take me long to see that the changes could all be happening at once because my boys needed me. I was home more in the evenings, so we had much more time together. Family dinner time has always been extremely important to me, and now we could do it more often. *Stay focused, Barbie.*

I had been making a difference in the lives of people in my groups, but right now leading my family needed to be my highest priority. Michael and Dalton had more than their share of maneuvering through difficult relationships, so it helped that I was home more for them. Life's busyness could so easily sweep me away, but God was having me be still.

And in reality, my new life was so amazing despite the struggles. Things were going great with Richard. We were spending more time together, and he was so much more open and attentive. Dalton quickly made friends in our new neighborhood and school. My schedule was improving. I was making more money. And with some help from my oldest son, Nate, Michael got his first truck. When I kept my focus in the right place, I could see God moving. I could also see how Richard's more consistent presence had a positive impact on my boys. He could talk guy stuff with them and help with the new truck. Boys need men in their lives to show them what it looks like to be men. Richard was an amazing example of a godly man.

Contentment

A couple months after moving to the new house, the boys and I were at home. Dalton had a friend over, and they were playing outside. Michael was in his room playing video games. I was in the kitchen cleaning up from dinner. Suddenly I was overcome with the most incredible spirit of joy. I began thinking, wondering—was anything missing in my life?

I could honestly say there wasn't.

As much as I would have liked for Richard to be with me in that moment, it was such a good thing to know that my life was already full . . . and I was content.

I am finally in an amazing relationship. I am not desperate or looking for someone to take care of me. I am content where I

am; everything else is a bonus. Richard and Daylee would just
add to our already blessed life.
—Barbie's Journal

ᗌᎾᗍ

My favorite time of year has always been the Christmas season. I am all about traditions and family time. But since my divorce, enjoying that time of year had been a bit of a struggle. Splitting time with exes and figuring out the holidays with Richard could be difficult.

But this year, one particular day, again it hit me. I had my tree up and a fire was in the fireplace. It was a rainy day outside, and I was baking cookies to take to church for my new single-mom group.

And all I felt was joy.

I was overwhelmed with God's love and favor. My pastor describes blessings as the tangible and intangible favor of God. I definitely was experiencing both. I had just been given some new furniture for my home. I received an unexpected check in the mail. And when I had a flat tire, the gentleman at the tire store gave me a new tire at no charge. The only explanation for all of that goodness was God.

Dalton told me one day, "The people in our lives are such a blessing to our family." Even at eleven, he could see God at work in our lives. This time of blessings upon blessings continues to be proof to me that it is never too late to make a new decision. It is never too late to move out of my comfort zone toward the new things God is calling me to. I am so grateful my decisions to trust in God have made a difference in my kids.

I loved that my boys and I were so happy, and I loved the sound of laughter in the house. My relationship with Richard continued to deepen as well. One Saturday night, as we were sitting in church, he placed his hand on my leg. It was such a simple gesture, but it spoke volumes about how far he had come. That simple touch was God's way of telling me he was answering my prayers.

*2012 looks like the year that Richard and I might get married.
I am going to have to continue to give that to God. Richard did
share that he has looked at rings! I love him so much!*
—Barbie's Journal

FINDING YOUR RIGHT COMBINATION

What Richard and I Learned About Moving Out of Our Comfort Zones

Richard and I had both taken steps to be more vulnerable with each other, but now we were learning to step outside our comfort zones in new ways. Ways that disrupted our routines, our daily lives, our families. These decisions were necessary for growing closer to each other and to exploring a new life—the life God was revealing to us day by day, one bit at a time. Once Richard made clear to me that he intended to pursue marriage, I needed to move toward him—literally. At the same time, Richard was learning that moving into a new life often means disruption, not just for us but also for the people closest to us. That can get very uncomfortable.

What God's Word Says About Moving Out of Your Comfort Zone

Have I not commanded you? Be strong and courageous. Do not be afraid; do not be discouraged, for the LORD your God will be with you wherever you go. (Joshua 1:9)

Trust in the LORD with all your heart and lean not on your own understanding; in all your ways submit to him, and he will make your paths straight. (Proverbs 3:5–6)

We know that in all things God works for the good of those who love him, who have been called according to his purpose. (Romans 8:28)

The Spirit God gave us does not make us timid, but gives us power, love and self-discipline. (2 Timothy 1:7)

As God shows you more Scriptures that relate to moving out of your comfort zones, write them on this page too.

ᖇᖇᖇ

Deuteronomy 31:8; Isaiah 42:16; 43:18–19; Philippians 4:6–7; James 1:22

Begin Your Own Process

- Is God calling you to move out of a comfort zone? Consider your spiritual practices, work, relationships, holiday plans, housing, and typical weekend plans.
- What is your biggest fear when stepping out in faith?
- How do you feel when you think about change? Are you expectant for change, or do you get anxious and fearful?

Begin today to pray about any move you believe God is calling you to make. Search out Scripture and seek the counsel of wise believers for guidance in making this decision.

PART 3

IT'S ALL HAPPENING

CHAPTER 10

Worth the Wait

Patience and Blending Families

"One and Only." Here we go!
—Adele Richard

Barbie

FOR THE FIRST TIME, AFTER PATIENTLY (okay, *mostly* patiently) waiting, I was hopeful that this Valentine's Day would be the night Richard would propose to me. It wasn't his MO to make elaborate plans for Valentine's Day, so I was thinking that just maybe he had something extra special planned. *A girl can hope.* I knew he'd been looking at rings, so I hoped he'd be getting around to it sooner than later. It had been a long time coming, and I wanted everything to be perfect just in case. A fabulous outfit. Nails done. A romantic booth booked at an expensive steakhouse. Check. Check. And check.

I was full of anticipation from the minute we sat down to our meal. We started our date with a delicious appetizer of wonderful cheeses, fabulous wine, and great conversation. *So far so good.* And the entrée that followed was the most amazing steak and lobster.

Now? Nope. Maybe he's waiting for dessert.

After we ordered dessert, Richard got up to go to the restroom. I was still holding out hope. *Maybe when he gets back?*

We enjoyed the fantastic crème brûlée and a cappuccino, and then it happened—he had a gift for me . . . that was in no way shaped like a ring.

What? Are you kidding me? An Adele DVD? I'll admit, Adele has a beautiful voice, and she is one of my favorite performers, but I was *so* disappointed. No matter how you slice it, a DVD doesn't hold a candle to a sparkling diamond! I couldn't believe I was spending the rest of an almost-perfect evening watching Adele sing on the TV at my house.

I was sad that the evening didn't end the way I had hoped. In spite of my efforts to hide my feelings, Richard could tell I was disappointed with how the night ended and asked me what was up. I finally fessed up that I had been expecting to get a ring. As it turned out, he had proposed to his ex-wife on Valentine's Day, so he didn't want to do that again. *Somebody should have told somebody.* Oh well, no matter what, it had been a fabulous night in every other way.

The following weekend I got a great surprise from Richard that sort of made up for the Valentine's Day disappointment. He signed us up for the Nearlywed/Newlywed class offered by our church to prepare couples for marriage. In my mind, this was a huge statement to me that Richard was ready to take some bigger steps forward in our relationship. I was overwhelmed with God's love and excited about the promise of having a life as Richard's wife—hopefully someday soon.

Richard

It's Time

I was falling more in love with Barbie with every passing day. I'd had time to experience how truly beautiful she was, both inside and out, and I found it increasingly hard to hold back my passion for her. We were spending time together pretty much every day, and she'd even started bringing lunch to my apartment since I worked from home. Awesome on one hand, not so much on the other. Having her around so often when we were alone made for a few too many close moments and challenged in a big way our commitment to wait for sex until after marriage. We would always catch ourselves before we slipped out of control, but we knew we had to become more intentional about our choices. We had to make the decision before the decision. We had come too far to bail, and we also knew that God wanted to use us to reach others.

We decided it was best to avoid being at home alone too often and agreed to have open communication about our plan for the evening. We knew what we were doing was unusual among divorced people, probably even among single people, and we hoped our example would encourage others to walk with God as they searched for the right person to become their mate. We had a large group of friends and family, including our kids, who knew our commitment and were testing our example. Under the mounting pressure to keep our desires in check, I'd realized it was time to make some choices about our future and put a plan in place. I'd been looking at diamonds for a couple of months and was now sure of what kind I wanted to get for her ring, and I had made the decision to buy it. What I loved about Barbie was that I knew she was going to love her ring no matter what, so I didn't have any problem choosing it without her input. Now it was just a matter of when and how to propose.

Our women's ministry was starting a series on purity. What if I could propose to Barbie in front of the whole women's group? I felt like getting a yes from them was a long shot, in part because no man had ever spoken at this women's event before now, but what the heck? I had nothing to lose, so I emailed the women's ministry leader. I shared that I wanted to pull off a surprise proposal to Barbie, wrapping it up with these words: "I know a man has never spoken at this women's event, so this is me being like Peter, stepping out of the boat. Hey, if you don't ever step out of the boat you'll never walk on water."

I hit send on the email. *Here we go.* And to my surprise, she replied almost immediately: "Absolutely. Let me get back to you."

Yes! It was so amazing to see God directing my steps with his perfect plan.

Barbie

"Are You Interested in Being Interviewed?"

I am always glad to attend women's ministry events. The leader called to say that we'd be discussing purity and asked if I'd be interested in being interviewed about my relationship with Richard.

Holy cow! I didn't even have to think about it. I had learned so much about myself and relationships in my walk with Richard, and I loved sharing about all that God had done in our lives through our commitment to obedience and dating his way. I was so excited to tell Richard my news. I called him as soon as I hung up, but he was out to dinner with a friend and couldn't talk. But he did say, "That is so awesome, Barbie. I am so happy for you."

It's all happening!

Richard

"Propose to the Girl Already!"

I was sitting at dinner with my old friend Gary the week after I got the go-ahead on my plan for asking Barbie to marry me. Gary and I had been friends since fifth grade, and we talked often. He'd been on my case for a while to marry Barbie and wasn't afraid to press me about it. "What are you waiting for?" he'd ask. "Propose to the girl already!"

I was excited that night to tell him I was finally ready to do it. After four years, I was asking Barbie to be my wife. We were in the middle of talking over how I planned to pull it off when Barbie called to tell me that she'd been asked to speak at the next women's event. She was over-the-moon excited to get the invitation, and I had to work hard not to do or say anything that would give away my plans. I wanted to knock her off her feet and leave her speechless when the moment finally came. She had been waiting on me to propose for a really long time. Now that it was finally coming, I figured she deserved something wildly romantic.

Barbie

Is This It?

I was so excited to have an opportunity to share with such a large group of women. Richard and I had come a long way since we'd met four years earlier, and we'd seen how we were serving as an example to the many people who had watched our story play out. I had come to understand that God wants his best for us, that obedience was not about rules and regulations or punishment but for our protection.

It had never been easy to live out our walk of obedience in daily life, especially when it was so countercultural among singles and even more so after divorce. But we'd done it. Who would have thought I would be standing in front of a room of about two hundred ladies talking about sex, or more to the point, not having sex? Only in God's economy would this happen.

On the afternoon of the gathering, I met with the leader to go over the plan for the evening. She explained that she would be asking another lady and me questions about our relationships before breaking into small groups for more discussion on sexual purity in dating.

I arrived in the chapel that night early enough to visit with all my girlfriends before the program started—my favorite part of any gathering. The leader asked us questions about how we met our boyfriends, why we made the decision to remain abstinent in our dating, and how we had been able to keep our commitment. Honestly, I have no idea what answers I gave to any of those questions, because the next few moments changed my life forever. As the announcer was preparing to release the ladies to their small groups, she suddenly introduced Richard.

"You have heard about Barbie's boyfriend, and I think you should meet him," she said. "Please welcome Richard Armenta." *That is awesome, but he isn't here.* Suddenly Richard was entering the room and coming toward the stage, waving as the ladies cheered. He began addressing the group.

"As many of you know," he began, "Barbie and I have been dating for about four years. I made the decision to date God's way back in April of 2003 as a commitment to be obedient to God in every area of my life, so we know just a little bit about the struggles of dating God's way. If there is anything I can add to what you all have already shared tonight, it would be this: You are more beautiful than you think you are. You are more valuable than you think you are. And anything worth having is worth the wait."

A million thoughts raced through my head. *Why didn't he tell me he was coming? That is so sweet. Should I sit down? Wait! Is this it?*

As he turned to me, it suddenly dawned on me. This *was* it—the moment I had been waiting for. The one I was never quite sure would come.

Richard went down on one knee, speaking the most beautiful words I'd ever heard: "With that said, Barbie, I want *you* to know you are more beautiful to me than you think you are. You are more valuable to me than you think you are. And you have definitely been worth the wait! Barbie, will you please marry me?"

After all this time, after all the doubt and the struggles to be obedient and follow God, I couldn't believe he was finally blessing me with the man of my dreams.

Richard was still on one knee in front of me, waiting for something—anything. I was in shock. I wish I could say that I cried or fainted, but I just stood there staring at him in disbelief. The room was roaring with cheers and applause, and I finally managed to hug him and whisper, "Yes, absolutely!"

I was so grateful that I had not given up and that I'd let things happen in God's perfect timing. I knew that only God could have orchestrated this most perfect proposal. It would change our lives, and it would also bring hope to a roomful of ladies. Hope that there are still good, godly men out there. Hope that it is not too late to make a new decision. I had never felt more blessed.

The next thing I remember, Richard was taking a bow and walking to the back of the room amid a standing ovation. I was still standing on the stage, holding the ring box, wondering if this had really just happened. A friend jostled me out of my fog, and I rushed to meet Richard in the back of the room. It was in that moment that I actually got my first look at the stunning ring he'd given me. It was absolutely perfect.

As we stood there together taking in the moment, I realized my phone was buzzing like crazy. *What in the world?* I couldn't resist taking a peek to see what was causing such a fuss. To my surprise, I saw a string of social media notifications lighting up my screen. Many of the women in the room were posting about the proposal. *Oh my goodness! I don't want my boys to find out about something this important online.*

As Richard and I headed out, I made a quick phone call to Michael and Dalton to share our news and tell them we would be there after stopping at Richard's sister's house. He had planned in advance for Daylee to meet us there to celebrate. We had so much fun that night recounting the story and taking pictures with Daylee. While we were there, we also took the opportunity to make our own social media post announcing the engagement.

> *Well, ladies and gentlemen, I am officially off the market!*
> *That's right, you heard correctly! This boy is engaged to Barbie!*
> —Richard's Facebook Post

Our next stop was home to see the boys. They were super excited, and Michael told me that if he could pick anyone for me, it would be Richard. Those were the words my mama's heart needed to hear. We were all going to be a family.

It's All in the Details

After such a long courtship, we did not see any need for a long engagement. As far as we were concerned, we'd waited plenty long enough and were ready to get on with married life. We both thought six months was enough time to plan a wedding, so we dove headfirst into making arrangements.

We wanted to keep our day intimate, with family and special friends who had loved and supported us along the way. There was only one venue on our short list—Allaso Ranch. The big day: Saturday, September 1, 2012.

Thankfully, Allaso was available, and I was excited to check off the first of many tasks that lay ahead. I asked Daylee and my friend Cindy to be my bridesmaids. Cindy had stood by me from the beginning, so it made perfect sense that she would stand by me on the big day. And I couldn't think of anything more special than to have my new daughter standing with me.

Richard would be asking my boys to stand with him also. While Richard and I were the ones getting married, we understood that all of us would be joining as a family too. We loved the idea of having everyone up there before God and our friends to see us come together.

The dress . . . what am I going to wear? I had already decided I didn't want to wear a traditional wedding dress. I mean, this would not be my first time down the aisle, and it didn't seem right to go with a foofy white gown. I did, however, want Richard to think I looked fabulous.

A few months earlier, I'd seen a singer on TV wearing this gorgeous red jumpsuit, and I loved it. I thought that in ivory it could be perfect for the wedding. The jumpsuit was high-necked and sleeveless with flared legs, and from the front, looked almost like a dress. I had no idea where I'd find what I wanted ready-made, so I showed a picture to a sweet friend from church who is an amazing seamstress. She agreed to make it for me. How could I help but think, *I am so blessed.*

So many things came together quickly. The venue, the attendants, my jumpsuit—and thanks to Richard's friends, we had a free condo for a week in St. Croix for our honeymoon. *God is so good!*

I found myself glancing at the ring on my finger to remind myself that this was not a dream. This was my real life.

I Did Not See This Coming

In the midst of all the wedding-planning fun, I hadn't expected to find myself sitting in a doctor's waiting room as Richard underwent a biopsy.

Cancer? Not one time had I ever considered something like this popping up as we neared our wedding day. I was not actually that worried about the outcome. I believed the results would be normal. Richard was young and healthy. Prostate cancer was something that happened to older men, right? So I sat, waiting, and I prayed and journaled to keep my mind from going to the worst scenario. Richard and I had waited so long to be married and to enjoy the benefits we'd denied ourselves during the years we dated. We had a wedding and a honeymoon ahead of us. I just couldn't let myself believe God would take away our future sexual intimacy with the devastating side effects that can result from treating prostate cancer.

Richard

The Test Is Inconclusive

Several weeks before I'd seen my doctor, I kept getting the sense that something was wrong. I hadn't had any symptoms or felt bad; there was nothing I could pinpoint. I just had a feeling in my spirit that I needed to get checked out, so I scheduled for a routine physical. With a lot coming up in the next few months, I thought I'd be better off getting an exam just to be sure everything was okay.

I loved my doctor. I'd been seeing him for years, and we had a great relationship. He had a way of putting me at ease, even for the dreaded prostate exam.

"Nothing unusual," he said, "Everything looks good."

It was what I had been hoping to hear, but deep down I still didn't have peace.

"Are you sure?" I asked him.

He said he didn't have any concerns, but we kept talking. I shared how I just had this feeling that something wasn't right. So there I was asking him to check again. This time he was careful to check for even the slightest irregularity. Sure enough, there was something—a tiny nodule on the right side of my prostate, so small he'd missed it the first time.

"How did you know there was something wrong?" he asked.

"I didn't," I answered, "I just felt something telling me to check it out."

"Well, you were right," he said.

We decided to test my PSA level and keep an eye on it. Following the first test, the levels looked good, nothing alarming, so we decided to test it regularly in case anything changed. If it did, we could take another step.

At some point in the process of my regular checks, my PSA level made a sudden spike. My doctor confirmed it was unusual and warranted a biopsy as a precaution. He recommended I schedule an appointment as soon as possible.

It was an uncomfortable week of waiting for the results for both Barbie and me. We didn't want to get the news that I had cancer, so we prayed and believed for the best.

When the doctor finally called, he told me that he had good news and bad news.

"Which do you want first?" he asked.

"I want the good news, of course," I told him.

As it turned out, the biopsy came back inconclusive. I didn't have cancer, but then again, I didn't not have cancer. My doctor thought maybe we needed to do another biopsy, and suggested I return again in a few months for a follow-up. It was possible that we'd detected something too early to really know what was going on. So I agreed to come back later for another look. *I can live with inconclusive. Inconclusive is not cancer. God's got this!*

Barbie

It's Flavor Night

I've always loved going to our women's ministry events and seeing all the ladies. This night was a special one—not quite like the one when Richard proposed, but one when I would have another opportunity to talk about our relationship. The women's pastor had planned to interview a panel of ladies about relationships and dating, and she had asked me to be a part of it. It would be a ladies-only chance to have a real conversation about relationships and sex. We answered various questions that the audience had sent in before the event, ranging from how to talk to your kids about sex to how often you should expect to have sex when you're married. (In case you're wondering, the response to that last one is about every four days.)

One of the questions posed to me was this: We are already engaged and have made a commitment. Why should we still have to wait to have sex?

My response, to everyone's surprise, was, "I texted in that question." The audience response was priceless. "Just kidding!" I said. "I've waited this long. Why would I take a chance now?"

Our pastor summed it up best: "You have had God's hand on 90 percent of your relationship. Why would you want him to remove his hand of blessing now?" When we sin, there is always some negative effect. It might not be obvious to others, but it's real all the same. It might be guilt, shame, break of trust, or in this case, maybe even pregnancy. Why would I willingly do that to myself and the people around me?

The last thing I had the opportunity to share was that it is not too late to start again. God's forgiveness of sin and his restoration of relationships are real. I want women to know that no matter where we are or where we have been, it is never too late to have all that God has for us.

I loved getting this opportunity. So many churches are silent on the topic of sex. I am grateful to be a part of a church that talks so openly, as God himself does in his Word.

Stay Focused on Jesus

Daylee attended the women's conference at church with me. She planned to spend the night with me, and then we would drive to meet Richard the next morning. My boys would be with their dad for the weekend. I was looking forward to spending time with just the three of us. It didn't happen as often for me and Daylee as it did for Richard and the boys.

Daylee and I had a great time at the conference and on the drive, but I noticed a change in her once we met up with Richard. And the reason suddenly became clear to me. This was a trip she and Richard had taken alone many times, and I could tell she wasn't sure how to handle having me there too.

Daylee was going through a lot of change. When Richard and I became engaged, her mom was going through a divorce. Richard was her constant—her North Star. She had always been able to count on her life with him to be a certain way. Now things were changing, and it wasn't easy.

I think even she might have even been surprised by how much it bothered her once we got engaged. I understood her feelings, but it was hard. I loved her, and it hurt to have her not want me there. I knew she felt she was losing her dad. He was not the first single dad I had met whose daughter was *the* woman in his life. It makes it difficult to be a couple when someone is already in that spot.

When we returned home, Richard and Daylee decided to make some time for just the two of them. Great idea, except they chose to do it by going to an out-of-town family weekend I had previously been invited to attend. I was heartbroken! I couldn't help feeling that Daylee and I were competing for first place in Richard's heart. I had accepted that I was second all the years we dated, but I thought things would be different once we were engaged. Richard kept assuring me, "Just wait until we are married." So I was supposed to trust that once we were married he would put me first?

My counselor and I talked through my feelings about Richard's decision. I was hurt and resentful, but I didn't want to get stuck there. I wanted to have a heart for Daylee's needs; however, I had needs too. My counselor explained to me that when you get engaged, you begin the journey of getting married, so when Richard made the decision to exclude me from the family weekend, it felt like hitting a wall. I chose to let go and tried to see what God was teaching me through this process. I knew it would be worth it on the other side.

In an effort to make the best of the weekend, I ended up spending an afternoon with all my boys. We enjoyed a fabulous lunch by a lake watching people paddleboard. It looked like so much fun.

After our meal, we walked outside, and someone asked me if I wanted to give paddleboarding a try. *Hmm. Should I?* The boys could see me thinking it over and warned me not to do it because I would fall in. Somehow their cautions felt like a dare. Despite my wearing jeans and a top, I decided to give it a try. I kicked off my shoes and got on the board just like I knew what I was doing.

I was a smidge shaky at first, wobbling around as I tried to gain my balance and stay dry. But it didn't take me long to get the hang of it, and I loved it. Mostly I was just so proud that I'd taken a risk and done it. For most of my life I had tended to play it safe. It felt good to take a risk and try something new.

This was what my life had become—a series of adventures that had me kicking off my shoes and stepping out into new faith. I could see now why God had used the story of Peter walking on water to bring me to him. He knew how I would need those principles in my life to grow my faith and stay focused on Jesus, not the storm around me.

Richard

God Keeps Showing Up in the Details

I was glad Barbie and I had allowed the time and space to build a strong foundation for our marriage, because I could see where the kids might throw a monkey wrench into our relationship, intentionally or not, as they dealt with the changes in their own lives. I was already seeing that blending a family would be tough work.

I noticed Daylee acting out in ways she never had before. She made it clear that she did not want Barbie to come between what she and I had. I knew this probably had to do with the many discussions we'd had about God and family and how I had always told her the spouse should come first and the children should come second in a marriage. I couldn't blame her for struggling with the thought of taking the back seat after having been number one in my life for almost twelve years. She didn't know how to be "us" any other way.

Daylee wasn't the only one struggling. Our marriage was going to be a big change for Barbie and her boys too. Michael and Dalton had been the men of the house and had looked after their mom for a long time. Now I was coming in to shake up their roles as well. Barbie and I would have to work hard to be patient and remember to be the adults when things got ugly—to find the fine line between understanding and respecting their feelings without letting our kids call the shots. The one thing I knew was that, through it all, God just kept showing up and growing us together. I wasn't sure we would find our way quickly, but I trusted we'd find it.

God kept showing up in the details of our life too. My commitment to the apartment ministry ended in June, but Barbie and I were not getting married until September. That created a bit of a housing issue for us.

Many people in our spot would reason that they would be getting married soon and use that as their justification for moving in together. But Barbie and I were into our no-sex-until-marriage commitment too deeply to give up now. More and more we'd come to realize that our decision to wait was not as much about us as it was about God and others. We would just have to figure something out.

That's when I got a phone call from Daylee's stepdad, Mark, who found himself in the process of divorce and was living alone in a house on Eagle Mountain Lake. It may seem strange, but he and I had become great friends over the years, and we kept in touch frequently. Mark had been watching my relationship with Barbie evolve, and even though he didn't attend church, he knew how important our commitment to dating God's way was to Barbie and me.

"Hey, Rich, I've been thinking. I know you're looking for a place to live for a few months before you and Barbie get married. I was wondering if you would like to come live with me at my lake house."

"Wow! Are you serious? Of course. I would love that."

What an answer to our prayers! Only God can do something like that.

During those months living with Mark, amazing relationships were built between me, Mark, Daylee, and Mark's daughter. Mark and I shared the same visitation weekends, so it was great fun to spend time together and with our kids. On top of that, Barbie and the boys joined us many weekends to hang out by the pool, enjoy cookouts, and go boating on the lake. God was growing us as a true family before we even started actually living together. We couldn't have asked for a better transition into what would soon become our reality.

Barbie

Where Are We Going to Live?

Like Richard, I too had a housing concern. My lease was almost up in Lantana, and we would need four bedrooms to house all our family once we were married. But considering the ages of our kids, we wouldn't need that many rooms for long, so we had already decided it would be best to rent for a while. We wanted to find a four-bedroom house in Flower Mound. This location would be close to my job; there would be good schools for the boys; and it wasn't too far from where Daylee lived. So we set out to find our perfect house.

The problem was, no houses matched our checklist and our price range. So after exhausting the available options, we shifted to plan B and started looking all over the Dallas/Fort Worth area. Again, no luck. The only houses close to where we wanted to be were too small. The thought of cramming everyone into cramped quarters left us feeling discouraged.

One day Pastor Owen, who would later marry us, came into my office at the church, and we talked about the challenges Richard and I were facing. He strongly encouraged me not to settle. He reassured me that God had the perfect house for us, and he prayed with me. He counseled me to pray specifically for what we wanted and to wait.

I prayed, but I didn't wait. I should have been really good at waiting by then, but I wasn't. Afraid that we wouldn't find a place we liked in the right location, I called my realtor and told her we wanted to put a contract on a small house.

But I didn't have peace that I was making the right choice. So that night, on the way home from dinner with some girlfriends, I called the realtor back and asked her to look one more time. Within a few minutes, she called back to say that a four-bedroom house had just listed in Flower Mound. Without even seeing it in person, I instructed her to switch our application fee to that larger house. I just knew it was our house.

While this was happening, Richard was serving at summer camp with his students at Allaso Ranch for the week. I managed to get a message to him that I had finally found our house, and he later told me that his cabin of boys, all high school students from Flower Mound, had prayed with him that we would get that house. God was so showing up for us!

FINDING YOUR RIGHT COMBINATION

What Richard and I Learned About Patience and Blending Families

I don't know about you, but one thing I don't pray for is patience. Why? Because I have always heard that when you pray for patience, God will give you opportunities to learn it. Regardless, it seemed God was using

Richard to teach me that trying to rush the process might get me what I *think* I want, but I can miss God's best for me this way. When I practice patience, it gives God room to work behind the scenes.

Blending families involves more than just you, your spouse, and your kids. You also have the exes and extended family. You are making a decision that affects the lives of many, and it takes patience to allow everyone to catch up to the change.

You maneuver one thing and then a new situation comes up that all of you have to work through. Blending is a process, not a one-time event. Patience, communication, and grace are all required. But we also have to remember that when the Bible says two become one, that still applies. The marriage is the primary relationship. Husband and wife are stronger together.

What God's Word Says About Patience and Blending Families

Listen to my voice in the morning, LORD. Each morning I bring my requests to you and wait expectantly. (Psalm 5:3 NLT)

If we look forward to something we don't yet have, we must wait patiently and confidently. (Romans 8:25 NLT)

Be completely humble and gentle; be patient, bearing with one another in love. (Ephesians 4:2)

For this reason a man will leave his father and mother and be united to his wife, and the two will become one flesh. (Ephesians 5:31)

Not that I have already obtained all this, or have already arrived at my goal, but I press on to take hold of that for which Christ Jesus took hold of me. Brothers and sisters, I do not consider myself yet to have taken hold of it. But one thing I do: Forgetting what is behind and straining toward what is ahead, I press on toward the goal to win the prize for which God has called me heavenward in Christ Jesus. (Philippians 3:12–14)

As God shows you more Scriptures that relate to patience and blending families, write them on this page too.

෬◉෬

Psalm 68:6; Proverbs 23:22; 15:1; Romans 12:12; Ephesians 6:1–3

Begin Your Own Process

- In what area of your life do you struggle the most with patience?
- What would it look like to have one big, happy family?
- What do you feel is the most important thing to remember when blending a family? (Remember, this doesn't only mean children. It could include other relatives and significant friends as well.)

When we want something different, we have to be different. We do not carry our old patterns into our new life. Spend some time visualizing and journaling what your new family could look like, and think about what steps you can take today to work in that direction.

CHAPTER 11

And Two Become One

God Is Love

I promise to love you with all my heart and to be true and faithful, patient and kind, unselfish and giving in this love.
—Richard

Barbie

I FEEL SO HAPPY WHEN I HEAR THE BEATLES sing that all we need is love. I am in love with love! What we usually think of when we think of love is relationships, marriage, and family. But Scripture tells us that God is love. In that case, the Beatles were spot-on: love—God's love—is indeed all we need.

I heard a sermon once that talked about having God's love flowing through your marriage, and I thought of how beautiful that seemed. At the time, after two failed marriages, I wondered if God could still do that for me. Now here I was, about to marry the man of my dreams.

I think most of us go through life thinking we will finally reach some state of perfection once we reach a certain destination—a new job, new relationship, more money, wedding day. I'm a hopeless romantic, if you haven't already noticed, and I went into our wedding weekend with faith that God would give us the perfect stretch of days that ended in our vows and extended into our married life. I wanted to think our trials were behind us. But wouldn't you know, Satan was right there, trying his best to throw a wrench into our plans.

The Big Day

It was 6:00 a.m., September 1, 2012, and I woke surrounded by towering pines overlooking a serene lake in one of my favorite places in the world—Allaso Ranch. That place embodies the serene Spirit of the Lord as the wind whistles through the trees and gently ripples the water that laps at the lake edge. My heart is always at peace when I am there. I firmly believe you cannot go there without experiencing the Holy Spirit. For Richard and me, there was no more meaningful place to celebrate the change in our lives and our new beginning. It was our wedding day.

A few of my girlfriends and I had arrived at Allaso in the early afternoon the day before the wedding. We wanted to get there ahead of everyone else to begin setting things set up for the rehearsal and wedding. Richard and Daylee were to join us that evening for the wedding rehearsal, followed by dinner at a nearby Italian restaurant on the lake. The drive was about two hours from our house, and I'd had about an hour's head start when I got a call from Richard.

"Do you have my car keys?" he asked.

"Of course not. I'm sure I left them on the counter."

I did leave them on the counter, right? Digging down in my purse, I touched something that felt like keys. *Oh, dang.*

"I'm so sorry, Richard. I do have them," I confessed. "What are we going to do now? I don't have time to turn around."

It wasn't bad enough that Richard wouldn't have a car to drive; the centerpieces, table decor, and my grandmother's Bible were all in the trunk of his car. *Now what?* Richard assured me he would handle it and see me there soon.

Once at Allaso, my friends and I set up everything we had on hand. Then I waited impatiently for Richard and Daylee to arrive with the rest. I was so nervous, and I felt terrible for taking the keys. The more I thought about it, the more anxious I became. *How could I have walked off with his keys?* All I could do was pray it would all be okay.

Richard

Murphy's Law

Life always seems to throw a few last-minute challenges to keep us on our toes. After all we'd been through just getting to our wedding, Barbie and I had both prayed for an uneventful final stretch heading into our special day. Satan, on the other hand, seemed to be working overtime to keep us stirred up and stressed.

I stood in the kitchen looking at the phone in my hand and shaking my head. Of all the days for something like this to happen! I had to think fast to figure out a solution to our problem. There was no way Barbie was going to let me show up for the wedding without all the things she'd stashed in the trunk of my car. She'd worked so hard to put everything together for our special day, and I wasn't about to tell her she couldn't have what she wanted literally hours before we were to be married.

As I was rolling all of the possible solutions through my mind, I remembered that I had an extra car key in the nightstand in the bedroom at the lake house—an hour away. I would never make it to the rehearsal dinner on time if Daylee and I went chasing around after it, so I had no choice except to enlist the troops for help. I called my brother-in-law, Ray, with instructions for him and my nephews to get in the house and retrieve the key. Daylee and I could go ahead with what we had in the borrowed Jeep I'd driven to my house, and I'd let the guys pick up the stash of wedding decorations and deliver them to Allaso as soon as they could.

By now, Daylee and I were running behind, so we quickly gathered the stuff we needed for the rehearsal and wedding and jumped back in the Jeep, pedal to the metal, bound for Allaso Ranch. I decided not to worry about the car and everything in it. Based on our history, I knew Ray and the boys would come through.

In addition to the car key challenge, I could tell all morning that Daylee wasn't her usual happy self. Alone in the car, it was even more obvious, but I was no longer sure what I could say that I hadn't already said to make her feel better. I knew my marriage was making her feel like our relationship was going to change. I'd reassured her over and over how much I loved her, but my words just couldn't overcome the weight of all the uncertainty she was feeling.

Daylee and I had discussions in the past about what a Christian marriage looks like: God first, then spouse, and then children. I couldn't change that, and I didn't want to change it. I'd waited a long time to find a woman like Barbie, and I was looking forward to having a friend, a lover, and a life partner. As close as Daylee and I had become since my divorce, she was growing up and would one day venture out into a life of her own. She could see the immediate change coming as Barbie and I united; what she couldn't see yet was the time that would soon come, as it should, when she would leave home to start a career or become a wife and mother. Then, without Barbie, I'd be left alone. These were the moments that made life.

This change in my life was just one more in a string of major changes for my daughter. She'd gone through my divorce with her mother; she'd gone through her mom's separation from her stepdad; and now I was about to marry Barbie—all in the space of twelve years. It was a lot to ask of a seventeen-year-old. I did my best to understand and to reassure my daughter that she and I were just fine. No one would come between us. No matter what, she would always be my daughter, and I would always be her dad.

I had hoped our two-hour drive to Allaso would give us time to talk about the wedding and all our mixed-up feelings before we got caught up in the festivities. Not a chance! Daylee put her earbuds in and sat closed off to me and the rest of the world. There was no getting through to her. I was so frustrated with her that I didn't know what to do. By now, I had no doubt that Satan was working overtime to try and ruin this day, but that would happen over my dead body. Instead, I made a conscious choice to walk by faith through this mess and believe for something better on the other side.

As I hoped, Ray and my nephews came through like champs and delivered the decor and the Bible that had been held hostage in the trunk of my car that day. It didn't happen without a few hiccups, but hey, they got the job done.

In spite of all the craziness preceding the wedding rehearsal and dinner, when I saw Barbie, she had never looked more beautiful in my eyes. I could not wait to see her in the outfit she'd chosen for the wedding. This woman made me happy, and I was so excited to start our new chapter in life together. For the first time ever, I felt I had a partner.

Barbie

The Rehearsal

Richard and Daylee arrived right on time for the rehearsal at 6:00 p.m. They had cut it really close and had no time to freshen up, but I was so happy to see them both. I knew it had been a stressful time for them, with all they had to do to get into the car. I felt terrible that we were off to such a rough start, but I looked forward to relaxing with them over a good meal and sharing the time with our family and friends. The decorations and Bible were still on the road somewhere, but Richard had promised that he would handle getting it all delivered, and I was trusting that it would all arrive just when we needed it. We went ahead with a quick run-through of the ceremony with Pastor Owen before making our way to the restaurant.

Unfortunately, the chaos of the day followed us to dinner. When we arrived, we were surprised to see the awkward arrangement of our tables. All our guests were seated in horseshoe fashion, and our table, the head table, had been set behind all of them. The setup totally removed Richard, me, and our kids from the rest of our guests. And by now it was too late to have the restaurant staff rearrange the tables. We were so bummed.

Richard and I were further disappointed when Daylee left our table to sit with her cousins at another table. I kind of didn't blame her; I mean, the table we were at felt so separated from our guests. But at the same time, it meant a lot to Richard and me to feel like we were finally becoming a family—all of us, including my boys and Daylee.

After dinner, my best friend and bridesmaid, Cindy, made a toast and presented Richard with a really long receipt as a "bill" for her time spent counseling me during the years we'd dated. Heaven knows I had spent many hours on the phone with Cindy, and across the living room from her, as I lamented the worries and shared the joys of dating Richard. It was supposed to be a really funny moment, but it somehow fell a little flat in the face of our stress. Richard and I should have been more joyful, but we felt there was something still to be resolved.

Richard

What Else Can I Say?

As the dinner ended and Barbie and I wrapped up to head back to Allaso, I was still disappointed that Daylee seemed so sad, or mad, or whatever she was. I knew things were tough for her, but I wanted her to be happy for me. I wished she knew how much her silence was killing me. She and I had come a long way through all we had been through over the years. We'd had so many late-night conversations and phone calls talking over all the things teenage girls think about and struggle with at that time in their life.

I mean, come on, with all the changes that have happened over the years, I've been your constant.

I couldn't help feeling like she was pulling away from me at one of the most important times of my life, when all I wanted was to draw nearer to her. I wanted to see her smile light up the room and make things all good between us again.

Barbie

The Night Before: The Ladies

When we returned to Allaso, the guys all went down to a cabin, and the girls stayed up at the main building. My friends and I changed into our pajamas and robes, and we hung out on the couches, laughing and recounting stories of my long courtship with Richard. I was so blessed as they each prayed over our marriage, but I was sad that Daylee continued to separate herself. Struggling with her own sense of loss, she had stepped out onto the deck to be alone.

My heart was broken for her, but also for myself. I felt so saddened by the lost opportunity to connect with Daylee and show her how much I loved her and how much I looked forward to having her as my daughter in my life. I wanted so much for the two of us to have a good relationship. Early on I believed we did, but now I just didn't know how to read her or how to help her through her own pain. I did the only thing I knew to do: I prayed that God would give her peace and change her heart.

Richard

The Night Before: The Guys

I was so disappointed in Daylee's behavior toward Barbie and me that night at the rehearsal dinner. I knew she was struggling, but a part of me wanted her to just get over it. I wanted her to be happy for us, but I wasn't going to make things worse with a confrontation. I decided to just let it go and prayed she would come around by the time of the wedding.

Back at Allaso, we said good night to the girls and headed down to the cabin where all the guys would be staying. Nate, Michael, and Dalton were having a great time together messing around and laughing. They were checking out their clothes for the wedding and wondering if their shoes looked good. Michael discovered that the vest of his suit was too small, and he went back and forth over whether he should wear it. I sat back and had the best time watching the boys be together. I had enjoyed getting to know them over the years, and I loved each of them for the person he was. I felt honored that God chose me to be a new spiritual leader in their lives.

As we were all getting ready to hit the sack that night, I went out on the patio of the cabin to pray over the wedding, Barbie, her boys, and especially Daylee. I knew the love we had for each other, and I knew beyond a shadow of a doubt that nothing was coming between us. I knew God was only adding to us.

When I went back in the cabin to say good night to the boys, I felt completely at peace, knowing that God had this in his hands.

The Big Day

The next day I woke up at the crack of dawn, left the boys sleeping, and headed over to the main cabin area where the girls were staying. I felt so good, and I truly believed God's hand was on me. The walk over was beautiful. The birds were singing, the sky was starting to show the sun's beautiful Texas color on the early morning clouds, and a touch of fog was rising off the lake as I crossed over the bridge. I sat down on a rock wall in front of the cabins to wait for Barbie to join me. We had planned this moment to meet so we could pray over the day before it got started.

We talked about the day ahead, and both of us seemed a little nervous. Here we were with our four kids getting ready to come together as a family, and while we felt we'd had more than our share of drama leading up to the day, we were full of hope. We prayed over the wedding, our guests, our new family, and for our future before going our separate ways to prepare for the day.

Barbie

The Bridal Suite

It wasn't long after I got back to the cabin that Daylee came to me. She told me that she had prayed the night before when she was out on the deck, and she was feeling much better. *God loves us so well!* I told her how glad I was and that I knew her dad would want to know, but she really had no way of contacting him since the cell phone reception was really bad on the property. It would have to wait until he arrived at the main building.

The next few hours went by quickly as we prepared for the ceremony. There was a lot of talking and laughing as the girls dressed and got their hair and makeup just right. The closer the time came, the more nervous and more quiet I got. By the time I was ready to put my outfit on, I found myself alone in the bathroom even though about eight of my girlfriends were talking over one another in the next room.

After all the fittings, the jumpsuit fit perfectly, and as I stood there, I had such a sense of peace come over me. *This is it.* We were finally here, and I was so glad I'd trusted God as he'd walked me through my journey with Richard. I was filled with joy.

"Ten minutes," I heard someone say, and suddenly the girls were rushing me to go downstairs. As we arrived in our "holding area," I was with Cindy and Daylee . . . until Daylee took off running toward the main building.

Richard

The Groom's Room

After praying with Barbie, I returned to the cabin to find that the boys were finally awake, and we started getting ready for the day. I could tell they were nervous, so I tried to lighten the mood, and we kidded around about the suits, how they fit, and especially Michael's one-size-too-small vest. I helped them with their ties. I knew their mom would think they were so handsome. I couldn't help but wonder how Daylee was doing, and suddenly I felt a sense of overwhelming peace.

The boys and I had all gathered in the main worship center's holding area with our pastor. Pastor Owen circled us around to pray before we got started. Owen prayed over me and Barbie, and in his wisdom, he also prayed over all the kids and asked that God have his hand on them to protect them in the blending of our families. Just as he finished praying, out of nowhere, Daylee came running around the corner. Like a linebacker in a football game, she hit me right in the chest and jumped into my arms. We both immediately started to cry and could not let each other go. With tears running down her face, she said how sorry she was about the way she'd been acting, and she told me she was happy for me. It was just what I needed to make the day perfect. Just as fast as she'd appeared, she was gone again.

Barbie

Mr. and Mrs. Richard Armenta

Acoustic guitar music echoed as my oldest son, Nate, walked me down the aisle. Our other three kids stood with Richard and Pastor Owen. Richard looked so handsome in his light-colored suit. The whole setting was beautiful, with the sunshine bright in a blue sky and shimmering off the lake in the background. As we approached the end of the aisle, Richard smiled and whispered, "Beautiful." Tears traced down my cheeks. This was, and still is, the happiest moment of my life.

The ceremony was absolutely perfect. Pastor Owen explained our reasons for choosing Allaso Ranch for our location, but even if he had not, our guests would have seen and felt the Spirit of God there the same way we did. We shared the vows we had written for one another, and there in front of all the people who mattered the most to us, we became husband and wife.

"May I present to you Mr. and Mrs. Richard Armenta," said Pastor Owen as we turned to face the crowd. It was all so surreal, and we loved how God was caring about every detail of our day. A sweet friend sang beautifully as we walked back up the aisle.

The ceremony was followed by a brunch reception with an oatmeal bar and a buffet of breakfast tacos. Everyone was talking and laughing, and I was overwhelmed with joy. Richard had chosen the perfect song for our first dance, "Your Precious Love" by Marvin Gaye and Tammi Terrell. It was the most incredible, heaven-sent moment to have the man of my dreams twirling me on the dance floor surrounded by all the people we loved.

☙❦❧

Richard and I had a two-hour drive back home in the borrowed Jeep. The drive went by quickly as we talked about the day and anticipated the night ahead.

We had decided to have a cookout at our new house that afternoon to spend time with our family and friends before heading off for our wedding night and honeymoon. There is nothing that Richard and I love more than family time, but even I had been a little hesitant about deciding to delay heading to the hotel. I mean, I had been waiting a long time for this night. But in the end I was so glad Richard convinced me to do the cookout. We all talked about the day, told stories, and laughed. I loved seeing how happy Richard was with all the people he loved the most around him.

Secretly, we were a little worried that everyone might forget this was our wedding night and stay a little too long. While we did not want to rush anyone off, we did have a time limit on the event. However, we worried over nothing. Right on time, everyone said their goodbyes, and we headed for the hotel. We were looking forward to spending our first night together at a fabulous hotel—the gift of a special friend.

"I Have Never Felt This Way Before"

We were greeted in our room with champagne and chocolate-dipped strawberries, which we enjoyed on our balcony as we talked about our day. Being together now took on new meaning, and we both wanted to honor the gift we'd be sharing as a married couple. I'll never forget when Richard said to me, "I have never felt this way before." He explained how he could feel God was doing something new in him, that he was doing something new in us. It was clear we were experiencing a spiritual and emotional connection that was different than either of us had ever felt.

What made his statement so significant was that he said it before we had sex. All along, I thought that our obedience had been about sex (or not having sex). But it was really about God being at the center of our relationship. Despite the fact that we had both been married before, and obviously both of us had had sex before, this was different. Neither of us had experienced the spiritual connection God was now blessing us with, and it was the most amazing feeling. The rest of our night was so romantic and had been so worth the wait! I suddenly knew what it meant when my friend Cindy used to say, "God will redeem your time." I felt like my life was brand-new and restored. Richard and I were seeing God do exceedingly abundantly more than we could have ever asked or imagined.

Sunday morning, Richard and I arrived at the airport bright and early for a 4:00 a.m. flight to St. Croix. I still felt in awe that I was finally Mrs. Richard Armenta. The journey here had seemed so long and incredibly hard at times, but I could look back and see just how much God had grown me, and us, in that time. *Now here we are married. Richard is being so attentive and calling me "babe," and I am loving every second of it!*

Some of our friends had gifted us with a stay at a beautiful little resort, and we were so excited to explore the property and the surrounding beaches in the days ahead. Between the two of us, Richard was the adventurer, but I had already decided to let loose of my cautious nature so I could enjoy my time in true "Richard" style.

We swam and snorkeled and soaked up the beauty of St. Croix and each other's company. Our week together went by all too quickly. Before we knew it, we were on a plane heading back to Dallas. We were ready to get home, see our kids, and begin our new life.

I had enjoyed seeing Richard so relaxed, but on the plane I could see the stress coming back. He said he wanted to make sure he was the best husband and stepdad he could be, and I was touched that he cared so much about it. I loved him so much, and I had never experienced this kind of unconditional love before. I was full of anticipation, expectation, and excitement, and I so looked forward to our future, believing the best was yet to come.

How Can God Let This Happen?

"It's cancer."

Sitting at my desk at work, I was in complete disbelief as I hung up the phone. Richard called to let me know his doctor had just confirmed our worst fears. The biopsy results finally came back, and he had been diagnosed with prostate cancer. *How can this be? Our marriage is only weeks old. After doing everything right, this is what happens?*

A million thoughts raced through my head. They caught it early. While he would likely recover, he could become impotent. For a short time, we let our thoughts go to *How could God let this happen?* We had waited all this time, and now we might not have sex again?

Richard quickly led us right back where we belonged, reassuring me and himself. "This is not the God we serve. We'll have faith and believe for complete healing," he announced. Of course, we realized bad things can happen, but we determined to focus on the healing we were praying for.

Walking in obedience does not ensure you won't face trials. You will deal with hard things. You just won't go it alone. Through our obedience and putting God first in our dating, God was ensuring that we would be stronger together. God was equipping us for the trials that he knew would come. Today Richard is cancer free and symptom free! We are amazed every day how God shows himself with his grace and favor.

The truth is, if Richard had been made impotent by cancer treatments, God is still good. We had built a foundation for our marriage that would have carried us through. Richard is my best friend, and God would have still been at the center. We will never regret our walk of obedience in dating. As I write these words, we have been married seven amazing years and counting, and we continue to put God first in our relationship and our family.

FINDING YOUR RIGHT COMBINATION

What Richard and I Learned About God's Love

God is love. This is what Scripture tells us. In my journey to finding the love and life I wanted, I ran right into the love I truly needed—God's love. This is the love that's everlasting. Only through God can we become whole and complete—free from guilt, shame, judgment, and people-pleasing.

It is only then that he can choose to bring a godly mate alongside you and then have God's love flowing through your relationship. The good news is, it is not the other person who brings the love—you are already loved beyond measure. Having a godly relationship is just one way to experience love. When you receive Christ, his love is already in you.

So what is the right combination? God gave me three words: courage, commitment, and faith. It's having the courage to be who God made you to be, the commitment to stay the course even when it is hard to see what God is doing, and the faith to trust in his ways.

God is a good Father. He loves you immensely, he has a good plan for your life, and his timing can be trusted. It is never too late!

Ladies, you are more beautiful than you think you are, you are more valuable than you think you are, and anything worth having is worth waiting for.
—Richard

What God's Word Says About His Love

Love is patient, love is kind. It does not envy, it does not boast, it is not proud. It does not dishonor others, it is not self-seeking, it is not easily angered, it keeps no record of wrongs. Love does not delight in evil but rejoices with the truth. It always protects, always trusts, always hopes, always perseveres. Love never fails. (1 Corinthians 13:4–8)

And now these three remain: faith, hope and love. But the greatest of these is love (1 Corinthians 13:13)

And so we know and rely on the love God has for us. God is love. Whoever lives in love lives in God, and God in them. (1 John 4:16)

This is love for God: to keep his commands. (1 John 5:3)

As God shows you more Scriptures that relate to his love, write them on this page too.

☙☙☙

Zephaniah 3:17; John 3:16; Romans 5:8; 1 Peter 5:6–7; 1 John 4:8

Begin Your Own Process

- What does it mean to you that God loves you?
- Do you think you can commit to dating God's way? Why or why not?
- What would it mean to you to live in freedom?

Take some time to look back over your notes in the "Begin Your Own Process" section of each chapter. Consider how far you've come in your relationships with God and others. Take time to thank God for the good things he has done, is doing, and will do in your life. This is a great time to start a gratitude journal. Beginning each day in gratitude makes it difficult to have a bad day. God blesses us in so many ways. It is up to us to return to him with gratitude.

We are praying for you as you continue to enjoy your own process. And we are so grateful you chose to let us share our journey with you and have made it a part of yours!
—Barbie and Richard

When you imagine your best life,
what do you see? An energetic, capable woman,
stepping forward into her goals? One who is
courageously living the life God created for her?

Is that who you see in the mirror today?

brave

Beautiful   Restored   Authentic   Vulnurable   Empowered

It's never too late to become all that God
designed you to be.

Join Barbie Armenta as she empowers women everywhere to
bravely live their most authentic and purposeful lives.

Visit www.rightcombination.net to find out more!